# PROLEGOMENA TO A GRAMMAR OF BASQUE

TERENCE H. WILBUR
*University of California*, Los Angeles

AMSTERDAM / JOHN BENJAMINS B.V.

1979

IN LIEU OF A PREFACE ...

The purpose of this study is to apply experimentally
the principles of recent grammatical theories to the facts
of the Basque language.  This study serves to test out
those principles and endeavours to discover the best form
for a grammar of Basque.

# CONTENTS

TABLE OF CONTENTS

\* \* \* \* \*

# ACKNOWLEDGEMENTS

I would like to thank my colleagues in the Department of Germanic Languages at UCLA for their support and encouragement in the completion of this work. I am also indebted to the unfailing patience of my typist, Marina Preussner, and to the understanding of the series editor, who followed the fate of this book with continued interest.

Los Angeles, California                                          T. H. W.
    August 1978

# I. INFORMAL PRELIMINARIES

## INFORMAL PRELIMINARIES

1.000 THE BASQUE PEOPLE. The Basque language is spoken in the provinces of Navarra, Guipúzcoa, and Biscay in Spain and in the districts of Labourd, Basse-Navarre, and Soule in the Department of Pyrénees Atlantiques in France. Speakers of Basque number about 500,000 in Spain and nearly 100,000 in France. This ferociously independent people has left its indelible mark upon the histories of France and Spain, indeed upon the history of the entire world. In the homeland, Basque energy has had a disproportionate influence upon the prosperity and success of those present-day entities of a political nature that share between them the seven provinces. It must be emphasized that Basque enterprise and toughness have also contributed mightily to the development of the New World. About 50,000 Basques live in the United States, particularly in California, Colorado, Idaho, and Nevada. The Basques in their great adaptability have turned out to be more Yankee than the Yankees.[1]

1.100 THE BASQUE LANGUAGE. The Basque language has always exerted an almost magical fascination upon European scholars. There, upon the European continent, surrounded by the all-too familiar Romance languages, a distinctly non-Indo-European language of uncontested antiquity continues to be spoken by about six hundred thousand people with a strongly marked cultural tradition, a colorful temperament, and a stormy history. This simple fact has caused a great deal of learned perplexity. Although there have been some rather engaging speculative excursions into lunacy, an extraordinary amount of worthwhile and conscientious scientific work has been carried out in the fields of Basque prehistory and linguistics. In fact, from the time of the earliest publications, works concerning Basque history, grammar, and lexicography have been consistently of the finest quality. Those works can

stand up honorably against the learned works of any nation.  The complete history of the Basque grammarians will one day provide a valuable
source-book of historical information for scholars in the field of
linguistic history and theory.

      1.200  BASQUE ORTHOGRAPHY.  While the elementary facts about the
world-languages such as French, English, and Spanish are either very
well known or easily ascertained, basic information about Basque is not
so easy to find.  In this section I shall attempt to give the uninitiated reader an informal guide to the exterior form of Basque and its
orthographical usages.  Like any other real language, spoken Basque
displays a great deal of dialect variation.  Literary practice in
that small land is just as varied.  I have chosen as the basis for this
grammatical study the literary dialect of Navarre and Labourd as described in Pierre Lafitte's *Grammaire Basque (Navarro-Labourdin Littéraire): Edition revue et corrigée* (Bayonne: Editions des amis du musée
basque, 1962).  Because I am seeking to define fundamental grammatical
operations, I shall within the scope of this work ignore dialect variations.  This is an artificial stance imposed against my otherwise
healthy inclinations by the practical limitations of this study.  It is
my conviction that only within an acceptable and satisfactory grammatical framework can dialect detail by given a meaningful form.  While the
written forms of Basque are rather variable, that variability is actually contained in such narrow limits that even the most striking individual usage is not at all difficult to interpret.  Basque orthographic
practice  is based primarily upon the usages of Western Romance, and,
in particular upon the usages of Spanish.  There are enough surface
resemblances between the phonetics of Basque and Spanish to make the
employment of those usages rather comfortable.  I must emphasize that
in this preliminary chapter I intend merely to provide the reader with
guideposts for the initial understanding of Basque forms and Basque
sentences. A critical treatment of the systematic phones and of the phonology of Basque must be reserved for a separate study.  Here, for instance, I shall overlook such weighty and difficult problems as palatalization and aspiration in Basque phonology.  It must be pointed out

that the matter of aspiration has been a hindering factor in the general adoption of a unified and modern orthography.[2] In this description
orthographic symbols will occur in italics, phones in square brackets,
and morphophonemic forms in small capitals.

　　1.201  As was mentioned above, aspiration is one of the thornier
problems of Basque phonology and dialectology.  In very general terms,
Basque dialects can be divided into aspirating and non-aspirating dialects.  These correspond to the dialects spoken in France and Spain,
respectively.  Aspiration, where it occurs, is indicated by orthographic *h*.  There is a certain amount of variation and inconsistency in the
indication of aspiration in the aspirating dialects.  For example,
*aphez* "priest" occurs alongside *apez* and *alhaba* "daughter" occurs
alongside *alaba*.

　　1.202  The orthographic symbols *p, t, k* represent the phones [p],
[t], [k], that is, voiceless stops, bilabial, alveolar, and velar,
respectively.  [k] is in some texts, represented by *qu* before *i, e,*
but by *c* or *k* otherwise.

　　1.203 The orthographic symbols *b, d, g* represent the phones [β],
[δ], [γ] intervocalically, that is, bilabial, alveolar, and velar voiced
spirants.  Initially the orthographic symbols represent the corresponding voiced stops, [b], [d], [g].  After liquids, *l* and *r*, the situation
is somewhat variable, being subject to individual and dialectical variation.  Sometimes the stop is heard and sometimes the spirant.

　　1.204  *tt, dd,* which are also written *t̄* and *d̄,* represent palatalized alveolar voiceless and voiced stops respectively, [ţ] and [ḍ].
It is to be noted that the very important process of palatalization
affects primarily the alveolar series.  Underlying *dd* is often realized
*j* [y], a palatal glide, in phonetic and orthographic representation.
Thus we find such pairs as *jantzen / dantzen* "dance" where a more consistent representation would be *ddantzen / dantzen*.

　　1.205  *m* and *n* represent the phones [m] and [n], voiced bilabial
and alveolar nasals, respectively.  Phonetic [m] is often written *n*
before a following bilabial, e.g. *zonbat* "how much" and *denbora* "time".

Sometimes this is morphophonemically justified.  Before a following
velar consonant *n* is realized as [ŋ], a voiced velar nasal, e.g.
*zango* [saŋgo] "foot". *ñ* , which occurs in some texts, represents a
pure palatal nasal, [ɲ].

1.206  *l* represents a voiced alveolar lateral, [l]. *ll* or *l̄* re-
represent palatalized *l* as [λ], a palatal voiced lateral.

1.207  *r* represents [r¹], an alveolar voiced flap. *ṙ* or *rr* represent [r], an alveolar voiced roll or trill.  The contrast of *r* and
*rr* is one of the well-known phonetic phenomena of Spanish.  *r* and *rr*
do not contrast preconsonantally and finally.  In these positions only
*r* is written.  No native Basque word ever begins with *r* or *rr*.

1.208  The sibilants and affricates offer the greatest phonetic
problems.  *z* represents a voiceless groove dorsal alveolar spirant [s],
which in some dialects is voiced medially.  *s* represents, on the other
hand, a voiceless groove apical alveolar spirant.  Some speakers retract
the apex to prepalatal position.[3] The distinction between *s* and *z* is
subject to some individual and dialect variation, but less than one
might suspect, for phonetic [s] is rather carefully distinguished from
phonetic [ṡ].  *x* represents [ʃ], a palato-alveolar slit spirant.  In
texts influenced by the French tradition, it is represented by orthographic *ch*.  It is the palatalized partner for both *s* and *z*.  *tz*, *ts*,
*tx* represent the corresponding voiceless affricates [ts], [ts], [tʃ],
respectively.  *tx* is the palatalized partner of both *tz* and *ts*.  In
texts influenced by the French tradition, *tx* is represented by *tch*.  In
texts influenced by the Spanish tradition, it is represented by *ch*.

1.209  *f* represents a voiceless labio-dental [f].  This phone or
systematic phoneme is a sore point in Basque phonology.  It has often
been repeated that [f] occurs only in borrowings from other languages.
This is not always so.

1.210  The orthographic vowel symbols *i, e, a, o, u* on the whole
represent the phones [i], [e], [a], [o], [u].  *e* and *o* would perhaps be
better described as pure mid-vowels, [E] and [ω].  In Souletine *ü* is
often written where it represents the mid-front rounded vowel [Ø].

*i, e* before a following vowel merge phonetically as [iy] and *u, o* merge
in the same position as [uw]. The orthographic digraphs *ai, oi, au, eu*
in general represent the diphthongs, [ay, oy, aw, ew]. In some texts
nasalized vowels are indicated by a circumscribed tilde, e.g. *ã*.
Occasionally in the texts we find vowels with a superscribed circum-
flex accent. This indicates a phonetically long vowel created by the
juxtaposition of two like vowels that has come about morphologically.
In this little sketch I have been deliberately careless of detail and
I have conscientiously avoided phonological interpretation.

1.300 SAMPLE TEXT. As a taking-off point for a discussion of
Basque Grammar, I have chosen the sentences of a short tale in the
dialect of Labourd recorded by Karl Bouda in 1917. The sentences of
this tale are of sufficient variety and complexity to permit a rather
expansive discussion of the major problems in Basque grammar. These
sentences will be supplemented by examples from Lafitte's *Grammaire,*
other grammatical works, and diverse literary sources. The sentences
will provide the newcomer to Basque with a short preview of how Basque
sentences are put together.

1.301  BI MANDOZAINAK "Two Mule-drivers"

a. *mundu huntan usu gerthatzen den bezala lehenago baziren bi mandozain.*

b. ###MUNDU##HUN#TA#N##USU##GERTHA#TZE#N##D#EN##BEZALA##LEHEN#AGO##
   BA#Z#IRE#N##BI##MANDO#ZAIN###

c. In this world as it often happens, there were once two mule-drivers.

1.302

a. *bakhotchak bazituzten zazpi mando.*

b. ###BAKOTX#AK##BA#Z#IT#U#Z#TE#N##ZAZPI##MANDO###

c. Each one had seven mules.

1.303

a. *merkhatuetarat joaiten ziren beren mandoak khargaturik.*

b. ###MERKATU#ETA#RAT##J#ÒA#TE#N##Z#IRE#N##BERE#N##MANDO#AK##KHARGA#
   TU#RIK###

c. They went to the markets, having loaded up their mules.

1.304

a. *Pariobat egin zuten, eta parioa galtzen zuenak bere zazpi mandoak galtzen zituen.*

b. ###PARIO##BAT##E#GI#N##Z#U#TE#N##ETA##PARIO#A##GAL#TZE#N##Z#U#EN#
A#K##BERE##ZAZPI##MANDO#AK##GAL#TZE#N##Z#IT#U#EN###

c. They made a bet, and the one who lost the bet lost his seven mules

    1.305

a. *batek irabazi zuen parioa, bainan ez chuchenean, zeren bertzea
trompatu baitzuen.*

b. ###BAT#EK##IRABAZI##Z#U#EN##PARIO#A##BAINA##EZ##XUXEN#E#A#N##ZER#
EN##BERTZE#A##TROMPA#TU##BAIT#Z#U#EN###

c. One won the bet, but not honestly, for he had duped the other one

    1.306

a. *bainan halere hunek bere mandoak eman zaizkon.*

b. ###BAINAN##HAL#ERE##HUN#EK##BERE##MANDO#AK##E#MA#N##Z#AI#Z#KO#N##

c. But nevertheless he gave his mules to him.

    1.307

a. *parioa galdu zuena aita familiakoa zen eta haurrez khargatua.*

b. ###PARIO#A##GAL#TU##Z#U#EN#A##AITA##FAMILIA#KO#A##Z#EN##ETA##
HAURR#E#Z##KHARGA#TU#A###

c. The one who lost the bet was the father of a family and was burde
with children.

    1.308

a. *etzakien, zer egin, ez, nola ethor bere etcherat.*

b. ###EZ##D#AKI#EN##ZER##E#GI#N##EZ##NOLA##ETHOR##BERE##ETXE#RAT###

c. He did not know what to do, nor how to go to his home.

    1.309

a. *hainbertze zuen phena bere gerthakariarentzat.*

b. ###HAIN#BERTZE##Z#U#EN##PHENA##BERE##GERTHA#KARIA#REN#TZAT###

c. He had so much remorse on account of the foolish thing that had
happened.

    1.310

a. *huna, zer egin zuen: bere etcherat joaiteko behar zuen zubi bat
trebesatu.*

b. ###HUNA##ZER##E#GI#N##Z#U#EN###BERE##ETXE#RAT##E#OA#ITE#N##BEHAR#
Z#U#EN##ZUBI##BAT##TREBESA#TU###

c. Here is what he did:  in order to go to his home, he had to cross a
   bridge.

       1.311

a. *eta deliberatu zuen gauren pasatzea zubi haren azpian.*

b. ETA##DELIBERA#TU#Z#EN##GAU R#EN##PASA#TZE#A##HAR#EN##ASPI#A#N###

c. And he decided to spend the night under that bridge.

       1.312

a. *gau erditan aditu zituen botz batzu.*

b. ###GAU#ERDI#TA#N##ADI#TU##Z#IT#U#EN##BOTZ##BATZU###

c. At midnight he heard some voices.

       1.313

a. *sorginak ziren Akhelarrerat heltzen.*

b. ###SORGIN#AK##Z#IRE#EN##AKELARRE#RAT##HEL#TZE#N###

c. There were witches coming to Akhelare.

       1.314

a. *batek egiten zuen fusta eta bertzeak husta.*

b. ###BAT#EK##E#GI#TE#N##Z#U#EN##FUSTA##ETA##BERTZE#AK##HUSTA###

c. One made a "whoosh" and the other a "wham."

       1.315

a. *han eman ziren dantzan tamburina soinuz.*

b. ###HAN##E#MA#N##Z#IRE#N##DANTZA#N##TAMBURINA##SOINU#Z###

c. There they began to dance to tambourine music.

       1.316

a. *aski gozatu zirenean, batek erraiten zuen:  holako etcheko andere
   eri da zazpi urthe huntan.*

b. ###ASKI##GOSA#TU##Z#IRE#N#E#AN##BAT#EK##ERRA#ITE#N##Z#U#EN##HOLA#
   KO##ETXE#KO##ANDERE##ERI##DA##ZAZPI##URTHE##HUN#TA#N###

c. When they had enjoyed themselves enough, one said: a certain
   Mrs. So-and-so has been sick these seven years.

       1.317

a. *egin ahalak oro eginik ere, ez dezakete senda.*

b. ###E#GI#N##AHAL#AK##ORO##E#GI#N#RIK##ERE##EZ##DE#ZA#KE#TE##SENDA###

c. Having done everything that can possibly be done, they cannot make
   her well.

1.318

a. *bainan ez dute sendaraziko, elizako borthan apho batek ahoan dagokan ogi benedikatu puchka bat hatcheman arte eta jan arazi arten andere hari.*

b. ##BAINAN##EZ##D#U#TE##SENDA#RAZI#KO##ELIZA#KO##BORTA#N##APO##BAT# EK##AHO#A#N##DAUKA#N##OGI##BENEDIKA#TU##PUXKA##BAT##HATX#E#MA#N## ARTE##ETA##E#A#N#ARAZI##ARTE#A#N##ANDERE##HAR#I###

c. But they will not make her well until they find a piece of sancti- fied bread that a toad is keeping in his mouth at the church door and until they have had that woman eat it.

1.319

a. *gure mandozainak eskutatu zuen ontsa, zer erran zuten sorginek.*

b. ###GURE#MANDO#ZAIN#AK##ESKUTA#TU##Z#U#EN##ON#TSA##ZER##E#RRA#N## Z#U#TE#N##SORGIN#EK###

c. Our mule driver heard well what the witches said.

1.320

a. *eta hek lekhuak hustu orduko, joan zen bere etcherat.*

b. ###ETA##H#EK##LEKHU#AK##HUSTU##ORDU#KO##E#OA#N##Z#EN##BERE##ETXE# RAT###

c. As soon as they had left the place, he went to his house.

1.321

a. *etzuen batere erran bere andereari, galdu zituela mandoak.*

b. ###EZ##Z#U#EN##BAT#ERE##E#RRA#N##BERE##ANDERE#A#RI##GAL#DU##Z#IT# U#E#LA##MANDO#AK###

c. He said nothing at all to his wife about his having lost the mules.

1.322

a. *beztitu zen aphur bat eta abiatu.*

b. ###BESTI#TU##Z#EN##APUR##BAT##ETA##ABIA#TU###

c. He put on some little thing and left.

1.323

a. *joan zen, joan, joan andere haren etcheari buruz hura hatcheman arte.*

b. ###E#OA#N##Z#EN##E#OA#N##E#OA#N##ANDERE##HA#RI##ETXE#A#RI##BURU#Z## HURA##HATX#E#MA#N##ARTE###

c. He went, went, went on ahead to the house of that sick woman until he found it.

    1.324

a. *azkenean arribatu zen berak desir zuen lekhura.*

b. ###AZKEN#E#A#N##ARRIBA#TU##Z#EN##LEKHU#RA###

c. Finally he arrived at the place he wanted.

    1.325

a. *eta galde egin, nahi ziotenez eman egoitza.*

b. ###ETA##GALDE##EGI#N##NAHI##Z#I#O#TE#N#E#Z##E#MA#N##E#GO#I#TZ#A###

c. And he asked whether they wanted to give him a place to stay.

    1.326

a. *erran zioten, piajant zela, eta othoiztu, utz zezaten han egoiterat*
   *zombait egun.*

b. ###E#RRA#N##Z#I#O#TE#N##PIAJANT##Z#E#LA##ETA##OTHOITZ#TU##UTZ##ZE#

   ZA#TE#N##HAN##E#GI#ITE#RAT##ZOMBAIT##EGUN###

c. He told them that he was a traveller and asked that they might let
   him stay there several days.

    1.327

a. *erran zioten:  baietz.*

b. ###E#RRA#N##Z#I#O#TE#N##BAI#ETZ###

c. They told him yes.

    1.328

a. *jakin zuen, etcheko anderea eri zela, eta asmatu, guziak egin*
   *zituztela nahiz sendarazi.*

b. ###E#AKI#N##Z#U#EN##ETXE#KO##ANDERE#A##ERI##Z#E#LA##ETA##ASMA#TU##

   GUZI#AK##E#GI#N##Z#IT#U#Z#TE#LA##NAHI#A##SENDA#RAZI###

c. He found out that the housewife was sick and guessed that they had
   done everything with the wish to make her well.

    1.329

a. *bainan ezin zutela deus iardets.*

b. ###BAINAN##EZIN##Z#U#TE#LA##DEUS##E#ARDETS###

c. But they could not attain anything.

    1.330

a. *gure mandozainak diote:  nahi duzuea ikhus dezadan nik ere?*

b. ###GURE##MANDO#ZAIN#AK##D#I#O#TE#NAHI##D#U#ZU#E#A##IKUS##DE#ZA#DA#
N##NI#K##ERE###

c. Our mule-driver said to them: Do you want me to see her too?

1.331

a. *behabada egin nezake zerbait.*

b. ###BEHA#BA#DA##E#GI#N##N#ZA#KE##ZER#BAIT###

c. Perhaps I can do something.

1.332

a. *sarrarazi zuten.*

b. ###SARR#ARAZI##Z#U#TE#N###

c. They had him go in.

1.333

a. *etsaminatu zuen ontsa anderea.*

b. ###ETSAMINA#TU##Z#U#EN##ON#TSA##ANDERE#A###

c. He examined the woman well.

1.334

a. *eta erraiten dio: orhoitzen zirea, duela zazpi urthe, botatu zinuela mespreziorekin eliza borthan ogi benedikatu puchka bat?*

b. ###ETA##E#ERA##ITE#N##D#I#O##ORHOIT#TZE#N##Z#IRE#A##D#U#E#LA##ZAZPI##
URTE##BOTA#TU##Z#IN#U#EN#LA##MESPRESIO#REKIN##ELIZA##BORTA#N##OGI##
BENEDIKA#TU##PUXKA##BAT###

c. And he said to her: Do you remember that seven years ago you threw away with disdain a piece of sanctified bread at the church door?

1.335

a. *erraiten dio baietz.*

b. ###E#RRA#ITE#N##D#I#O##BAI#ETZ###

c. She told him yes.

1.336

a. *hemen geroztik hunat, apho batek dagoka ogi benedikatu puchka hura ahoan.*

b. ###HEMEN##GERO#Z#TIK##HUN#RAT##APO##BAT#EK##D#AGO#KA##BENEDIKA#TU##
PUXKA##HURA##AHO#A#N###

c. From that time to this, a toad has been keeping that piece of sanctified bread in his mouth.

1.337

a. *eta etzire sendatuko hura jan artean.*

b. ###ETA##EZ# Z#IRE##SENDA#TU#KO##HURA##E.#A#N##ARTE#A#N###

c. And you cannot become well until you have eaten it.

1.338

a. *senharra partitu zen berehala mandozainarekin.*

b. ###SENHARR#A##PARTI#TU##Z#EN##BEREHALA##MANDO#ZAIN#A#REKIN###

c. The husband left immediately with the mule-driver.

1.339

a. *azken hunek erran zioen bezala, hatcheman zuten aphoa harri baten*
   *azpian bere ogiarekin.*

b. ###AZKEN##HUN#EK##E#RRA#N##Z#I#O#EN##BEZALA##HATX#E#MA#N##Z#U#TE#

   N##APO#A##HARRI##BAT#EN##AZPI#A#N##BEREN##OGI#A#REKIN###

c. As the latter had told him, they found the toad under a stone with
   their bread.

1.340

a. *hartu zioten eta ekharri etcherat.*

b. ###HAR#TU##Z#I#O#TE#N##ETA##E#KARR#I##ETXE#RAT###

c. They took it (the bread) away from it (the toad), and took it home.

1.341

a. *garbitu zuten ontsa eta eman jaterat etcheko andereari.*

b. ###GARBI#TU##Z#U#TE#N##ON#TSA##ETA#E#MA#N##E#A#TE#RAT#ETXE#KO##

   ANDERE#A#RI###

c. They cleaned it well and gave it to the housewife to eat.

1.342

a. *eta hura sendatua izan zen berehala.*

b. ###ETA##HURA##SENDA#TU#A##I #ZA#N##BEREHALA###

c. And she was healed immediately.

1.343

a. *phentsa zazue hekien alegrantzia.*

b. PENTSA##ZA#ZU#E##HEKI#EN##ALEGRANTZE#A#==

c. Imagine their joy!

1.344

a. *nausiak nola baitziren hainitz aberatsak, senharrak erran zion mandozainari.*

b. ###NAGUSI#AK##NOLA##BAIT#Z#IRE#N##HAINITZ##ABERATS##AK##SENHARR#
AK##E#RRA#N#Z#I#O#N##MANDO#ZAIN#A#RI###

c. Since the man and wife were rich enough, the husband said to the
mule driver.

1.345

a. *galda zezok nahi zituen guziak eta izanen zituela.*

b. ###GALDE##ZE#ZA#K##NAHI##Z#IT#U#EN##GUZI#AK##ETA##E#ZA#N#EN##Z#IT#
U#E#LA###

c. Ask for all the things that he wanted and (he said) that he was
going to have them.

1.346

a. *mandozainak ihardetsi zion, ontsa kontent zitakela, balitu zazpi*
*mando, bazituela galduak haimbertze.*

b. ###MANDO#ZAIN#AK##E#HARDETSI#I##Z#I#O#N##ON#TSA##KONTENT##Z#IT#U#E#
LA##GAL#DU#AK##HAIMBERTZE###

c. The mule-driver answered him that he could be very happy if he
should have seven mules, for he had lost that many.

1.347

a. *etcheko nausiak erraiten dio: zazpi mando berriz zirela harendako.*

b. ###ETXE#KO##NAGUSI#AK##E#RRA#ITE#N##D#I#O##ZAZPI##MANDO##BERRI#Z##Z#
IRE#LA##HAR#EN##DAKO###

c. The man of the house said to him that there were again seven mules
for him.

1.348

a. *hitzeman zaizkon zazpi mando ere eta bertze aldiz segurki aski diru*
*bertze zazpiren erosteko.*

b. ###HITZ#E#MA#N##Z#AI#Z#KO#N##ZAZPI##MANDO##ERE##ETA##BERTZE##ALDI#
Z##SEGUR#KI##ASKI##DIRU##BERTZE##ZAZPI##REN##EROS#TE#KO###

c. He promised him seven mules too and besides that surely enough money
to buy another seven.

1.349

a. *gure mandozaina ontsa kontent zen.*

b. ###GURE##MAND#ZAIN#A##ON#TSA##KONTENT##Z#EN###

c. Our mule-driver was very happy.

> 1.350

a. *nola ezbaitzen espantutua, berriz hasi zen bere komertzari.*

b. ###NOLA#EZ#BAIT#Z#EN##ESPANTU#TU#A##BERRI#A##HASI##Z#EN##
BERE##KOMERTZARI###

c. Since he was not proud, he began his business again.

> 1.351

a. *ikhusten zuen ardura bertze mandozaina, bere mandoak ebatsi zaizkona.*

b. ###I#KUS#TE#N##Z#U#EN##ARDURA##BERTZE##MANDO#ZAIN#A##BERE##MANDO#
AK##E#BATS#I##Z#AI#Z#KO#N#A###

c. He often saw the other mule-driver, the one who had stolen his mules from him.

> 1.352

a. *bainan hau etzen hurus gehiago bere hamalau mandoekin.*

b. ###BAINAN##HAU##E##Z#EN##HURUS##GEHI#AGO##BERE##HAMALAU##MANDO#EKIN###

c. But he was not happy any more with his fourteen mules.

> 1.353

a. *eritasun batek lothu zituen.*

b. ###ERI#TASUN##BAT#EK##LOT#TU##Z#IT#U#EN###

c. A disease had befallen them.

> 1.354

a. *eta jautsi jautsiak ziren lauetara.*

b. ###ETA#E#AUTS#I##E#AUTS#I#AK##Z#IRE#N##LAU#ETA#RA###

c. And they were gradually reduced to four.

> 1.355

a. *lasterrik etzaion bihi bat.*

b. ###LASTERR#IK##EZ##Z#AI#ON##BIHI##BAT.

c Quickly not a single one was left for him.

> 1.356

a. *ethorri zen bertze mandozainaren atchemaitera eta galdatu nola egin
zuen aintzinean bezenbat mandoren izaiteko.*

b. ###E#TORR#I##Z#EN##BERTZE##MANDO#ZAIN#A#REN##ATCH#E#MA#ITE#RA##ETA#
GALDA#TU##NOLA##E#GI#N##Z#U#EN##AINTZIN#E#A#N##BEZEN#BAT##MANDO#
REN##E#ZA#ITE#KO###

c. He went to find the other mule-driver and asked how he had done it,
   to get as many mules as before.

   1.357

a. *bertzeak erran zion:   huna, holako zubi azpian jakin diat, nola*
   *hatchemanen nituen ene mandoak.*

b. ###BERTZE#AK##E##RRA#N##Z#I#O#N##HUN#A##HOLA#KO##ZUBI##AZPI#A#N##E#
   AKI#N##D#I#A#T##NOLA##HATCH#E#MA#N#EN##NIN#TU#EN##ENE##MANDO#AK###

c. The  other one said to him:  Look, under a certain bridge I learned
   how I was to get my mules.

   1.358

a. *hik ere jakinen duk zerbait dudarik gabe.*

b. ###HI#K##ERE##E#AKI#N#EN##D#U#K##ZER#BAIT##DUDA#RIK##GABE###

c. You too will learn something without any doubt.

   1.359

a. *gure gizona badoha.*

b. ###GURE##GIZON#A##BA#D#OA###

c. Our man goes.

   1.360

a. *gau erditan ethortzen dire sorginak, harrama handitan atabal eta*
   *tamburina soinuz.*

b. ###GAU##ERDI#TA#N##E#TORR#TZE#N##D#IRE##SORGIN#AK##HARRAMA##HANDI#
   TA#N##ATABAL##ETA##TAMBURINA##SOINU#Z###

c. At midnight the witches came with great noise and with the music
   of the tambourine and drum.

   1.361

a. *oro arras kontent ziren eta eman ziren dantza ta zabaletan egiten.*

b. ###ORO##ARRAS##KONTENT##Z#IRE#N##ETA##E#MA#N##Z#IRE#N##ETA##E#MA#
   N##Z#IRE#N##DANTZA##TA##ZABAL#ETA#N##E#GI#TE#N###

c. All were very happy and they began to do the dance and mightily.

   1.362

a. *gero batek dio:   holako etcheko anderea sendatua izan da.*

b. ###GERO##BAT#EK##D#I#O##HOLA#KO##ETCHE#KO##ANDERE#A##SENDA#TU#A##I#
   ZA#N##DA###

c. Then one says: A certain Mrs. So-and-so has been healed.

    1.363

a. *izan behar da norbait, hunat heldu denik guk zer erraiten dugun eskutatzera.*

b. ###I#ZA#N##BEHAR##DA##NOR##BAIT##HUN#RAT##HEL#DU##D#EN#RIK##GU#K## ZER#E#RRA#ITE#N##D#U#GU#N##ESKUTA#TZE#RA###

c. There must have been someone who comes here to listen to what we have said.

    1.364

a. *behar dugu miatu zubi hunen azpian.*

b. ###BEHAR##D#U#GU##MIA#TU##ZUBI##HUN#EN##AZPI#A#N###

c. We must look under this bridge.

    1.365

a. *denak badohazi eta atcheman dute gure mandozaina, ez dakiena non gorde.*

b. ###D#EN#AK##BA#D#OA#Z#I##ETA##ATCH#E#MA#N##D#U#TE##GURE##MANDO## ZAIN#A##EZ##D#AKI#EN#A##NON##GORDE###

c. They all go and they find our mule-driver who does not know where to hide.

    1.366

a. *batek jo zuen eta bertzeak uchatu.*

b. ###BAT##EK##JO##Z#U#EN##ETA##BERTZE#AK##UXA#TU###

c. One hit him and the other pushed him.

    1.367

a. *hola erabili ondoan botatu zuten urera.*

b. ###HOLA##E#RABIL#I##ONDO#A#N##BOTA#TU##Z#U#TE#N##URE#RA###

c. After pushing him around this way, they threw him into the water.

    1.368

a. *eta han akabatu zen gure mandozain ohoina.*

b. ###ETA##HAN##AKABA##TU##Z#EN##GURE##MANDO#ZAIN##OHOIN#A###

c. And there our thieving mule-driver ended.

    1.369

a. *bertzea aldiz bizi zen aberats eta hurus bere familiaren erdian.*

b. ###BERTZE#A##ALDI#Z##BIZI##Z#EN##ABERATS##ETA##HURUS##BERE##
   FAMILIA##REN###

c. The other however lived rich and happy in the midst of his family.
   1.370

a. *dembora hartan bizi nintzen etche ttiki batean zubi haren aldean.*

b. ###DEMBORA##HAR#TA#N##BIZI##NIN#TZEN##ETCHE##TTIKI##BAT#E#AN##
   ZUBI##HAR#EN##ALDE#A#N###

c. At that time I was living in a little house near that bridge.
   1.371

a. *eta galdu ziren arizan nintuen mandozainaren leinuak.*

b. ###ETA##GAL#DU##Z#IRE#N##ARIZA#N##NIN#T#U#EN##MANDO#ZAIN#A#REN##
   LEINU#AK###

c. And the descendants of the mule-driver I mentioned were lost.
   1.372

a. *geroztikako berririk ez dakit, bainan uste dut hainitz sorgin berek*
   *igorri zuten izaitekotz Ameriketan gaindi bere pekatuen pagatzerat*
   *galtzagorrieren gana.*

b. GERO#Z#TIK#A#KO##BERRI#RIK##EZ##D#AKI#I##BAINAN##UTS#TE##D#U#T##
   HAINITZ##SORGIN##BERE#K##I#GORR#I##Z#U#TE#N##I#ZA#ITE#KOTZ##
   AMERIKE#TA#N##GAIN#DI##BERE##PEKATU#EN##PAGA#TZE#RAT##GALTZA#
   GORRI#E#REN##GANA###

c. I do not know anything new since then, but I believe, the same
   witches have rather sent many by way of America to the devils to pay
   for their sins.

    1.400 TRADITIONAL BASQUE GRAMMAR. Basque differs very strikingly
from other languages spoken in Western Europe. Many of our implicit
assumptions about grammar that are so helpful in the study, say, of
English, German, French, or Spanish simply do not work. One of the most
common explicit assumptions about Basque grammar that causes more harm
than good is the notion that the "case" system of Basque can be presented
and explicated after the fashion of the grammars of the inflecting classical languages, Latin and Greek. The explanation for this intellectual
syndrome is self-evident. However, that explanation does nothing

to remove the difficulties that a paradigmatic presentation creates.
As a matter of fact, the paradigmatic arrangement of the "declension"
of any particular Basque noun disguises more than it reveals. Even a
casual inspection of one of these paradigmatic arrangements of forms
discloses one simple fact:  a paradigm is unnecessary. Latin, for example, has a number of differing declensions while Basque has but one.
Latin has a limited number of possible inflexional forms for each possible paradigm whereas Basque seems to have a variable number of them,
depending upon the grammarian who makes up the list. With a little
industry one can invent an enormously long paradigm for any particular
noun in Basque, for Basque by a regular process of derivation adds affix
to affix to affix. The notion of a paradigm is from the outset much too
clumsy for the discussion of Basque. A painful example of the paradigmatic fallacy is to be found in Ormaechea and Oyarzabál's *El lenguaje
vasco* (1963:30 *et passim*) where we find, for instance, such wondrous
declensional endings as *-renganako*. This monster is not a declensional
ending at all, but a series of affixes introduced by regular grammatical
processes into the nouns phrase:  *-ren + gana + ko*. For this assortment
of declensional endings the reader will find such labels as *directivo
indefinado, directivo terminal, impulsivo,* and other terminological odd-
ments.  These labels represent unnecessary baggage that obscures the
grammatical processes of Basque.  The kind of ordering they introduce
into the grammar is misleading and specious.

     1.500  THEORY OF GRAMMAR.  Any theory of grammar and, conse-
quently, any treatment of a language-particular grammar is concerned
first of all with the determination of just how sounds, produced by the
human voice or represented on writing materials, and meanings, present
in any communicative situation, are joined. These two, sound and meaning, alone comprise the real and tangible facets of human speech.  Any
steps or components "discovered" between these two concrete manifesta-
tions are abstractions--albeit often very convenient ones--created by
the linguist.  Such abstractions are at present best formulated by <u>rules</u>.
Rules represent in succinct form the regularities discovered in linguistic behavior, predicting and determining how the speakers of any partic-

cular language will transform meaning into sound and vice versa.
Recently a great deal of effort has been expended in extrapolating from
the rules of language-particular grammars the rules of all grammars,
i.e. the parameters of a universal grammar. We can say that willy-nilly
the application of any model of grammar to a specific language is also
an essay in universal grammar. The various *components* of a grammar
determined in the investigation of a language are sets of rules applying
to appropriate subsets of grammatical abstractions. The components,
their ordering, and their appropriate blocks of rules are not arrived at
in a simple inductive fashion, for the grammarian, consciously or uncon-
sciously starts out his investigation with a model, a hypothetical, preliminary, tentative scheme that serves as a blueprint for the production
of the finished work. That model will be hypothetical in that it represents the trained and intuitive guess of the linguist at what will best
account for meaningful speech activity, preliminary in that it must be
constantly revised in detail, and tentative in that it may not be able
to capture the significant generalizations aimed at.

The Western tradition of grammar, developed and cultivated for centuries in the schools, has provided for grammarians and specifically for
the grammarians of Basque a model to present raw grammatical facts and
to place an interpretation upon them. The exterior form of a grammar
according to this model was immediately comprehensible to the literate
world. Basque grammarians before all others were acutely aware of how
awkwardly the facts of Basque fit into this model. Traditional grammar
is presented according to a word-and-paradigm model whose primitive
terms of classification were the *partes orationis* and some fuzzy notions
about the functions of inflected words, e.g. subject-of, object-of, past
tense, etc. This dictionary-entry kind of presentation leaves most of
the significant generalizations to the intuition of the uninitiated
scholar. For one thing, a paradigm in Basque can be extended to prodi-
gious lengths. A listing of all the possible forms, consequently, explains nothing of grammatical interest. Basque grammarians were not the
only ones to feel dissatisfied with the inherited tradition, whatever
its great insights may have been. The general discomfort among all

linguists eventually gave rise to the generative-transformational movement in the study of grammar, initiated, according to current historiography, with the publication of Noam Chomsky's *Syntactic Structures* in
1957. Since that time generative grammar has been brought to a hitherto
unrealized state of refinement. Never before could the grammarian face
the object of investigation with a more coherent theory. That coherence
has spurred the opposition in turn to sharpen and make conscious its
aims and methods. Thus, a kind of dialectic, internal and external, has
created an atmosphere in which the fundamental problems can be fruit-
fully debated both at the philosophical level and at the practical level.
Any critique of the movement will have to take to task not so much the
not-yet-completed and insufficiently developed programs as two basic
impediments to complete clarification: (1) the superstitions, i.e. metaphysical presuppositions, inherited from Western grammatical tradition;
(2) the insufficiencies of a purely sentence-based grammar.

It must be emphasized that the refinement of the concept of rule,
always present in the history of grammar, made possible the general
acceptance of generativity as the central operational reality of language production and interpretation, for with a finite set of rules and
a more extensive, but still finite, number of lexical items the human
being can create an infinite number of well-formed sentences and readily
participate in the formation of longer, more complex language structures,
such as monologues, dialogues, narratives, etc., anything that can be
called in the broadest sense a *text*. At the same time, the human being
can with equal readiness interpret any of these products of language
activity, be it ever so novel. Therefore, the discovery of rules and
their formalization is the principal aim of the investigation of a particular language. The form of the rules, the entities or functions to
which they apply, and their exhaustiveness in accounting for and predict-
the course of sentence-and-text production and interpretation must be
the major focus of this essay. The basic assumption behind this en-
deavor is, of course, that the speaker of a particular language has in
the course of his own development internalized these rules that we so
earnestly attempt to extract.

1.501.   GENERATIVE GRAMMAR.   It is appropriate at this point to
lay out in rough plan the scheme of a generative grammar.  As a working
hypothesis the generative grammarian asserts the universal applicability
of his model.  Every application of it is accordingly an empirical
examination of the model, for he is trying it on for size.  Generally
five components are proposed for the model:  the *lexicon*, the *categorial*
(*phrase structure*) *component*, the *transformational component*, the *phonological component*, and the *semantic component*.  The lexicon and the
categorial component are frequently considered together as the *base component*.  The lexicon contains all the available formatives in the language under study, providing each item with a lexical entry describing
its phonological semantic, and syntactic properties.  This latter entry
also contains rules for the internal structuring of the lexicon, morphology, morpheme structure rules, and allomorphy.  The categorial component contains the rules for the generation of the base phrase markers
and for the insertion of lexical formatives, constrained by strict sub-
categorization and selectional restrictions.  The rules of this component require as categorial designators the primitive terms, Verb (V),
Noun (N), Adjective (Adj.), Adverb (Adv.), Determiner (D), Auxiliary
(Aux.), and Conjunction (Conj.), the definitions of which are at this
point necessarily ostensive.  Within the categorial component the
phrase markers provided with the lexical formatives make up the deep or
underlying structures of all the sentences of a particular language.
The phrase markers display certain functional relationships among its
constituents, such as *Head of Phrase*, *Subject of Verb*, *Object of Verb*,
*Indirect Object of Verb*.  The transformational component relates the
deep structures to or maps them onto surface structures.  The phonological component relates these surface structures to the phonetic substance of the sentences of any particular language.  The semantic component interprets the deep structures, deriving them from appropriate
semantic representations.

In this foreshortened account of the generative model, I have
passed blithely over important and disputed points, for this introduction is not intended to be a theoretical critique of generative theory.

In the essay proper I intend to resort to explication by example and to
introduce step by step modifications and criticism of the model.  The
model that this essay ends up with differs in many significant ways from
that of the greater number of generativists.  In recent literature,
Standard or Extended Standard Theory is most succinctly summed up in Ray
Jackendoff's $\overline{X}$-Syntax: *A Study of Phrase Structure* (1977).

1.502  AIMS OF THIS GRAMMAR.  This essay is devoted to the experi-
mental application of one form of generative grammar to the nominal
system of Basque.  More exactly it is a study of the set of affixes
that are attached to nouns, noun phrases, and nominalized phrases, or,
in terms of phrase structure grammar, to any string dominated by a node
marked N.  Thus, this essay is primarily concerned with the categorial
component.  Given these limitations to the study, I am obliged to set
aside extensive discussion and interpretation of questions of phonology,
morphology, pronominalization, and verb inflection.  When description
and discussion of these extremely important topics is necessary for the
elucidation of particular sentences or classes of them, I shall without
excuse provide an analysis, often in the form of excurses within the
text.  A number of raw, but necessary facts about the language will
also be presented in this abrupt fashion.  This will not detract from
the basic aim of this experiment, which is to capture some generalities
that will ultimately lead to the formulation of a qualitatively satisfy-
ing grammar of this intriguing language.  Therefore, I have named this
essay, *Prolegomena to a Grammar of Basque.*

# II. CONSTITUANTS, CATEGORIES AND BASIC PROBLEMS

# CONSTITUENTS, CATEGORIES, AND BASIC PROBLEMS

2.000  The first sentence of the tale reads:

1. *mundu huntan usu gerthatzen den bezala baziren lehenago bi mandozain.*
   As it often happens in this world, there were two mule-drivers.

Our linguistic experience tells us that an immediate constituent analysis of this sentence will reveal its lexical formatives and their surficial order, which will be representative for the whole language. This graduated breakdown reveals the basic terms from which ever higher units of order and their permutations can be reconstructed.  Each determined constituent is labeled in traditional terminology.

2.001

a. *mundu huntan usu gerthatzen den bezala* | *baziren lehenago bi mandozain*
   sentence:  subordinate clause | independent clause

b. *baziren lehenago* | *bi mandozain*
   independent clause:  predicate | subject

c. *bi* | *mandozain*
   subject:  numeral | noun

d. *baziren* | *lehenago*
   predicate:  verb | adverb

e. *(hura) mundu huntan usu gerthatzen den* | *bezala*
   subordinate clause:  relative sentence | subordinating conjunction

f. *(hura) mundu huntan usu gerthatzen da* | *en*
   relative sentence:  sentence | relative ending

g. *(hura)* | *mundu huntan usu gerthatzen da*
   sentence:  subject | predicate

h. *mundu huntan usu* | *gerthatzen da*
   predicate:  adverbial phrase | verb

i. *mundu huntan* | *usu*
   adverbial phrase:  adverb of place | adverb of manner
j. *gerthatzen* | *da*
   verb:  participle | auxiliary

   2.002 A bisecting process leads to a provisional hierarchy of
constituents within the sentence. This apparently inductive method
actually begins in the middle with data already processed by four centuries of orthographic practice and by our own innate, imperfectly
formulated, grammatical knowledge. By carrying the procedure further,
we arrive at a rough morphological analysis for each word. Admittedly,
no principle for distinguishing word from morpheme has as yet been
established.

   2.002

a. *mundu hun* | *tan*
   world this     in
   adverb of place:   noun phrase | inessive termination
b. *mundu* | *hun*
   world      this
   noun phrase:   noun | demonstrative
c. *usu*
   often
   adverb of manner:   adverb
d. *gertha* | *tzen*
   happen     ing
   participle:   verb root | participial termination
e. *da*
   is
   auxiliary:   intransitive copula
f. *en* | *bezala*
   which    as
   subordinating conjunction:   relative | conjunction
g. *bazire* | *en*
   they be     past
   verb:   intransitive copula | past termination

h. *ba* | *zire*

   positive    they be

   intransitive copula:  positive prefix | copula

i. *lehen* | *ago*

   form-     -erly

   adverb:  adverbial root | comparative suffix

j. *bi*

   two

   numeral

k. *mandozain*

   muledriver

   noun:  compound noun

l. *mando* | *zain*

   mule    keeper

   compound noun:  noun | noun

    2.003  With every binary cut a set of surface dependency rèlation-
ships have been established that can be defined as *head of construction*
and *complement*, or the modified term and its modifier. *Subject* | *predi-
cate* is an example of a basic relationship revealed by such a cut.
Tradition would have it that this particular relationship is *the* primary
grammatical function in sentence formation.  A basic sentence, then, consists of two terms, a verb, the head, modified by a noun  phrase, the
complement.  (In the parallel terminology of logic, we may speak of a
function and its arguments.)  Undoubtedly, one of the fundamental mis-
conceptions of traditional grammatical analysis is the often unconscious
assumption that the nominal subject is the head of the sentential construction, while the predicate is the complement, the modifying element.
This observation gives a firm foundation for the assumption of the cen-
trality of the verb in sentence grammars.  All other constituents must
serve as modifiers of the verb or as modifiers of its modifiers.  By its
very physical nature, human language requires a linear ordering of the
two terms, either *Modifier-Modified* or *Modified-Modifier*.  Whether this
linear ordering of constituents prevails at the deepest level of sentence formation is subject to investigation.  And, too, despite the

schemes of the typologists, which have been so popular of late, it is
questionable whether one order or the other operates absolutely in the
surficial linearization of categories and their constituents in any particular language.

2.004  What is most unsatisfactory in the immediate constituent
analysis above is the nature of the labels attached to the constituents
in the course of that analysis.  They represent a mixture of functional
and categorial notions.  The theoretical and practical difficulties that
arise in such practice have been spelled out by Chomsky in *Aspects of
Syntax* (1965:71).  The potential confusion can be avoided by the use of
tree-diagrams, useful devices that allow the analyst to indicate functional relationships configurationally in a manner where the nodes are
given only categorial names, e.g. S, NP, VP, etc.  The diagram indicates
a purely functional notion, e.g. *subject-of*, *object-of*, by placing it
in a configuration.  That is to say, the functional notion *subject-of* is
shown on the diagram by the fact that it is right-most and immediately
dominated by the node S.  Thus, function or grammatical relation is indicated implicitly and remains assumed and undefined.

The precise definition of "grammatical function" or "grammatical
relation" (or, in other words, just how one term modifies another term),
is a basic problem in the construction of an ultimately explanatory
theory of grammar.  It is no exaggeration to say that all grammatical
arguments circle around this problem.  Certainly all of the industry
expended in the search for the parameters of universal grammar will be
without issue until an answer is formulated that is so compelling that
all must accept it.

In actual practice, the functional terms with their implicit, but
vaguely defined assumptions have proved to be so powerful that all syntactic operations can be explained in terms of them.  Somehow, when the
analyst ascertains the subject of or object of the verb, he understands
something at the most primitive level.  So basic are these functional
notions that they were appropriated by generative grammar from traditional grammar.

In Figure 1, there is presented a configurational diagram of the

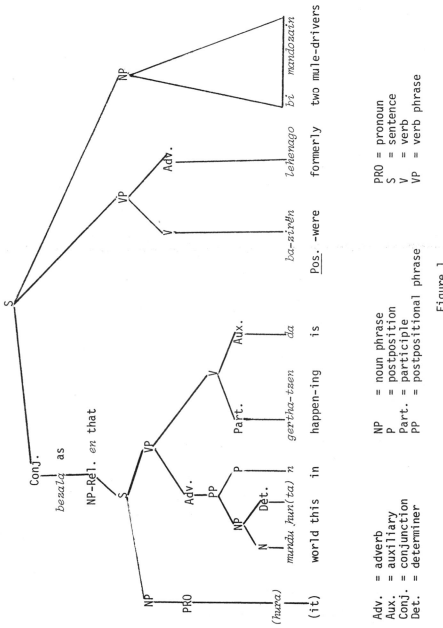

Figure 1

Adv. = adverb
Aux. = auxiliary
Conj. = conjunction
Det. = determiner

NP = noun phrase
P = postposition
Part. = participle
PP = postpositional phrase

PRO = pronoun
S = sentence
V = verb
VP = verb phrase

structure of the first sentence of the folk-tale. Here the functional relationships of the constituents appear in the form of branches on the tree. This analysis, really a slightly more sophisticated version of a grade-school parsing, shows us the complexity of the sentence. It shows us that the clause ending in *bezala* "as" is a complete sentence *embedded* as a modifier in another sentence. This shows the primary order of constituents in a Basque sentence, modifier-modified. In traditional terms, *bezala* is the head of a subordinate or subjoined clause. Subjoining turns out to be just one of the ways in which one sentence is *embedded* in another. This process is the major source of recursiveness in natural language grammar and the main topic of this essay.

2.005 The diagram in Figure 1 is intended to show a number of basic features of the surface grammar of Basque sentences. First of all, Basque can be characterized as a predominately suffixing or postpositing language. This characterization in no way damages the claim that the prevailing ordering of categories is modifier-modified. Reading left to right in sentence 1, we observe in the first adverbial noun phrase, *mundu huntan*, the general order of categories in all noun phrases: N, *mundu* "world"; Det., *hun(ta)* "this"; P, *-n* "in". The last element is often described as the termination of the *inessive case*. If the category Adj. should occur in any noun phrase, it is placed between N and Det., e.g. *mundu eder huntan* "in this beautiful world." This analysis gives us leave to reconsider the common notion of what a modifier is. (In the course of this essay I shall bring arguments against another commonly held opinion, viz. that *-n* is an inflection in the manner of the case endings of Latin.) This phrase is followed by another adverbial noun phrase, *usu*. Unlike the preceding phrase, it occurs in invariable form, i.e. without a postpositional marker. That such a marker has been deleted in the course of derivation is one conceivable interpretation. Thereupon follows a verbal phrase, *gerthatzen den*. Phrases of this form are often designated in this essay as *verb complexes* (VC). This term makes easier the description of the behavior of the Basque verb, for the greater number of verbs are composed minimally of two elements, a non-finite form of the lexical verb (participle, radical infinitive, infin-

itive) plus an auxiliary that incorporates pronominal indications of
ergative, neutral, dative, and allocutive noun phrases.  Allocution consists of a marker for the sex and social status of the person addressed.
The non-finite form *gerthatzen* is composed of these elements:  *gertha*, a
verb radical "happen", *-tze*, a nominalizing suffix "happening", and *-n*,
the inessive postposition.  The full form can be interpreted literally
as "in (the) happening."  This non-finite form is always followed in unmarked order by the auxiliary.  Here the auxiliary takes the form *da* is
generally interpreted as "it is."  The realized form *den* represents a
fusion of *da* and *-en*, the general relativizer, required here by the sub-
ordinating *bezala*.  The independent verb, *baziren*, as required by the
form of the verb complex, consists of two parts:  *ba-*, the positive prefix, which substitutes for the non-finite verb in this existential use,
and the auxiliary *ziren*, which incorporates indicators of third person
neutral, third person plural, and past tense.  The unitary adverb "for-
merly" lacks the postpositive marker.  It is made up of two parts:  *lehen*
"first" and *-ago*, the comparative suffix.  The noun phrase *bi mandozain*
consists of the numeral *bi* "two" and the noun, *mandozain*.  Indefinite
noun phrases containing a cardinal numeral take no indication of the
plural in contrast to *mandozainak* "the mule drivers," which has suffixed
indications of definiteness, *a*, and plural, *k*.

    2.006  The second sentence of the text (Figure 2) introduces two
important matters.  The first of which is the optional realization of
independent pronouns and the second of which is the *ergative case*,
which will be discussed at length in the following section.
2. *pariobat egin zuten.*
    They made a bet.
The surface realization of this sentence contains no noun phrase that
would indicate the "logical" subject of the verb.  The realization *heiek*
*pariobat egin zuten* is perfectly well-formed, but the demonstrative form
is contextually superfluous.  The presence or absence of independent
pronouns in Basque sentences is a matter of stylistic or contextual
variation.  That is to say, independent pronouns are subject to what
appears to be optional deletion.  In any case the content (case, number,

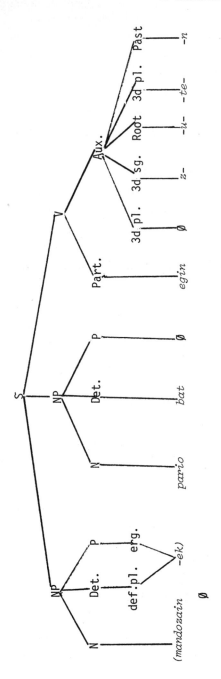

Figure 2

person) of that pronoun is clearly indicated in the incorporating
auxiliary.

   2.007  One of the thornier problems of Basque grammar and, inci-
dentally, of the general theory of syntax is revealed in the second sentence, for we meet the ergative case.  This case has been the focus of
considerable interest and dispute in recent grammatical literature.[4]  It
must be observed that periodically those linguists who aim at determining the universals of grammar rediscover this bothersome case in any
number of language stocks throughout the world.  Basically, the discussion and dispute revolve about the determination of the functional meaning of the traditional concepts of *subject* and *object*.

   In Figure 2 a constituent analysis of sentence 2 is presented,
displaying only what is represented in terms of surface formatives and
their categorial content.  This diagram does not indicate the functional
relationships that subsist between the noun phrases and the verb.  As
noted above one noun phrase must be interpolated in order to account for
the pronoun  reflexes on the auxiliary.  In the diagram I have inserted
a full noun phrase rather than a pronominal form.  That noun phrase must
contain, i.e. by suffixed *-ek*, a postposition that is labeled "definite
ergative plural."  This particular postposition is one of the few in
Basque where the morphological analysis is not transparent, i.e. where
we might speak of a true inflection.[5]  The second noun phrase, realized,
has no suffix.  It is unmarked or, if one wishes, it is marked by zero-
inflection as in the noun phrase *bi mandozain* in sentence 1.  Any person
trained in our grammatical tradition will be compelled to choose one of
the noun phrases in sentence 2 as the subject of the verb.  The second
noun phrase must fulfill the role of direct object.  We say, therefore,
that this is a transitive sentence or that *egin* is a transitive verb.
This stands in contrast to sentence 1 that has no second noun phrase and
is therefore intransitive.  This interpretation is arrived at not so
much because intuition dictates it, but because we are the recipients of
a powerful grammatical tradition that makes the distinction *transitive-
intransitive* seem to be quite natural and unforced in the treatment of
any grammar.  In the course of this essay, I hope to show that this dis-

tinction is in fact unnatural, distorting the real facts of Basque grammar. The implicit and, therefore, metaphysical assumption that every
verb must be transitive or intransitive leads to endless perplexities in
the interpretation of the immediate data of Basque. It forces the grammarian to create such spurious subcategories as deponent verbs (in
Basque grammars, those verbs that occur with only an ergative noun
phrase, that are "intuitively" intransitive), indirect transitives,
transitive verbs used intransitively and vice versa, as well as verbs
that are "optionally" transitive or intransitive. Obviously, there is
something unsatisfactory about this categorization.[6]

2.008  In Figures 3 and 4 we find two alternative analyses of the
functional relationships of the two noun phrases that assumes the validity of the traditional conception. Both have been defended at length
in Basque literature. Figure 3 represents the conservative view, dictated by the intuitive choice of the logical subject. This can be
characterized as the active theory of the Basque verb. Figure 4 represents the opposing theory of the Basque verb, the passivity theory.
This theory has been propounded and employed by notable scholars, Hugo
Mario Schuchardt (1893) and René Lafon (1943).[7] One of the principal
supports of this theory is the fact that Basque displays no passive constructions in the Indo-European sense. Claims that Basque does have
passive sentences are unsubstantiated by fact.[8]

2.009  The opposition of the two theories lies in determining
which noun phrase is chosen to be subject of the sentence. The first
theory says in effect that the subject of an intransitive verb is unmarked while the subject of the transitive verb is marked by ergative
-k, and its direct object is unmarked. This situation is the definition
for what the syntactic literature of linguistics calls "an ergative language." Anyone schooled in the European tradition will find the notion
contradictory in that the unmarked case, often called *nominative*, serves
as subject in one case and object in the other, because the underlying
assumption of the close relationship between morphology and function is
violated. In order to designate the unmarked case, I have chosen from
Basque grammatical literature the term *neutral case*. Many grammarians

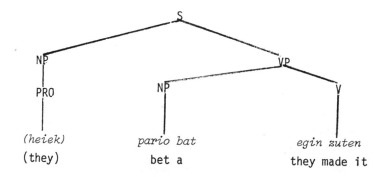

Figure 3

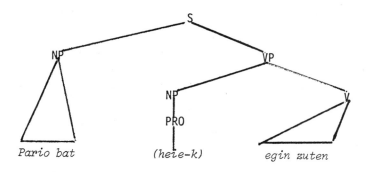

Figure 4

call it the *absolute case*.  The second theory preserves unit of morphology and function, claiming that the unmarked form is the subject of the
sentence and that the ergative marker is an agental suffix.  All transitive sentences are parallels to Indo-European passive sentences.  Sentence 2 must be interpreted "A bet was made by the mule-drivers."  This
fits in well with the PS model in that in the first rewrite, S → NP +
VP, the unmarked NP is directly dominated by S, while marked noun phrases,
e.g. *mandozainek*, are dominated by VP.  Transitive and intransitive sentences gain structural identity.  This was an honest attempt to discern
a consistent meaning for the puzzling ergative case, leaving the neutral
case unmarked and unexamined.  This step toward the establishment of a
principled basis for the explanation of ergativity was exhausted in the
strained invention of paraphrases of Basque sentences by means of
strange French and German passive forms, e.g. Schuchardt's explication
of Luke 15:11, *Gizon batek zitven bi seme* "Mann einem-von sie-wurden
gehabt-von-ihm zwei Söhne," instead of a straightforward "Ein Mann hatte
zwei Söhne" (1923: 1) or Lafon's interpretation of a sixteenth-century
root-inflecting verb *eztemayo* as "il n'est pas donné à lui par lui"
(1943 II, 41-42).  The term *passive* thus involves us in a terminological
riddle, for a grammar so conceived ends up with a passive voice and no
active voice.  Schuchardt asks the meaningless question, "Does [Basque]
have an active verb?  To this he gives the answer, "The transitive verb
of Basque is conceived passively" (1893:2).  A grammar resulting from
this sort of analysis is a translation grammar inasmuch as the structure of one language is explicated in terms of artificial equivalents in
another.

    2.010  One of the bases for the attraction of the passivity theory
was never made explicit.  Inspection of Basque sentences reveals that
nouns marked ergative are characterized by a semantic feature [+ ani-
mate] or by metaphor [+ animated].  The noun phrase marked thus seems to
be perceived as an animate agent (instigator) of the action contained
in the verb.  This makes the relationship between noun and verb meaningful rather than empty, being dictated by the presence of a transitive
or intransitive verb.  The situation is reversed.  The classification

of a sentence or verb as transitive or intransitive is determined not by
the meaning of the verb but by the presence or absence of an NP marked
for ergative at one point in the derivation of the sentence.  The terms
*transitive* and *intransitive* thus possess only a slight amount of descriptive usefulness for the grammar of Basque.  In order to demonstrate this
rather radical point of view, let us examine a pair of sentences that
will illustrate the point very clearly:

7. *gizona oihanean galdu da.*

   The man is lost (has gone astray) in the forest.

8. *gizonak oihanean galdu du.*

   The man has lost it in the forest.

I posit these trees for the deep structure of each sentence in Figures
5 and 6, respectively.

   2.011  A casual inspection of Basque sentences shows that morphologically this language relies heavily upon suffixing.  In terms of a
dependency description the complement precedes the head of the construction.  Therefore, the terms used above, *postposition* and *post-*
*positional* phrase are apt to our purpose inasmuch as they indicate the
order of elements in the surface description of a sentence.  The other
term that might strike the reader as slightly idiosyncratic is the
term *verb complex*.  This term is also chosen for an immediately evident descriptive reason.  The Basque verb is morphologically far more
complicated than the verb of any Indo-European dialect.  (This fact has
induced many comparativists to seek out resemblances with the so-called
polysynthetic languages of North America.  This activity is often engaging, but seldom productive.)  The greater number of Basque inflected
verbs are realized in two parts, a verbal root with its relatively few
modifications and an auxiliary with its more numerous and rather complicated modifications.  In addition, there is also a very small class of
root-inflecting or primitive verbs in which all modifications are ap-
plied directly to the verbal root.  The verbal auxiliary contains morphemic indications of negation, tense, mood, aspect, ad well as pronominal elements that indicate concord with what tradition calls the
subject, the direct object, the indirect object, and the allocutive.

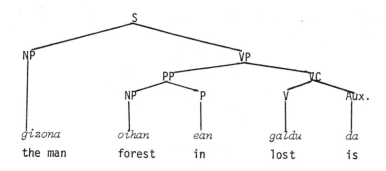

Figure 5

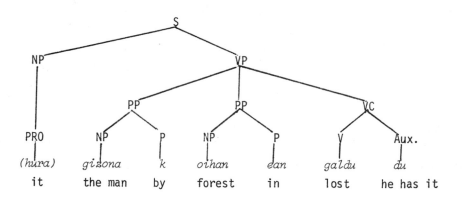

Figure 6

Definitions:

    P  = postposition (termination)
    PP = postpositional phrase
    VC = verb complex

The last term in this fairly long list requires some explanation. *Al-locution* refers to indications of the number, sex, and relative social standing of the person to whom a particular sentence is addressed. These indications occur in every inflected verbal form in an independent clause throughout a particular stretch of discourse. Rather subtle social considerations dictate the use of the allocutive forms. Needless to say, the surface conjugations of Basque verbs tend to be very elaborate when they are listed systematically in the fashion of a Greek or Latin grammar. This very fact accounts for the obsession of some Basque grammarians with the verb and its multitudinous realizations, sometimes--it must be added--to the detriment of the rest of the sentence. By way of illustration, I must point out that l'abbé Inchauspe's important and exhaustive grammar of the Basque verb, *Le verbe basque* (1885 Paris) encompasses 500 densely printed large quarto pages of non-repeating paradigms.

2.012  In the analyses of sentences 7 and 8 provided in Figures 5 and 6, it immediately becomes evident that a configurational analysis of these two sentences is in some way deficient. In Figure 6, it would appear that the PP dominating *gizonak* is equal grammatically to *oihanean* owing to the fact that they are both simply PP's dominated by the VP. However, removal of *oihanean* from deep structure leaves us with a grammatical sentence, differing from the original only in the amount of information it conveys. Removal of *gizonak* and its node leaves a non-sentence or, under the best of circumstances, quite a different sentence. That is to say, the functions of the two PP's are quite various. The first and most obvious difference between them is one of optionality. This fact requires the establishment of a hierarchy of postpositive phrases. In order to establish such a hierarchy, the nodes in the derivation must receive labels with ranked functions. In short, they must receive a syntactically valid classification. We find ourselves adding an element of meaning, a semantic criterion, to the classification of functions. Traditional terminology, unrefined as it is and impressionistic, provides some clues to the appropriate labels. For instance, *oihanean* might be labeled "postpositional adverb of

place" and *gizonak* "the complement of the agent." As noted above, the
first PP might also be described as "contingent" and the latter "necessary." The postposition that occurs or does not occur with the NP
*gizona* has its syntactic effect too. In sentence 7 *gizona* occurs in
the neutral case, i.e. without an overt postposition. In this case
the verbal form realized is "intransitive." In sentence 8 the same NP
realized with the ergative postposition triggers the appearance of a
so-called "transitive" verbal form. Therefore, the nominal forms are
not to be explained in terms of the verb class. On the contrary, the
markers on the noun phrase, the postpositions, determine the inflec-
tions on the verbal form.

2.013 We can sum up the problems discussed thus far under three
different headings:  (1) *tradition*, (2) *transitivity and subject*,
(3) *immediate constituents and phrase structure*.

2.0131 Tradition provides us with a fairly efficient means for
the analysis of sentences in particular languages. In general the
scheme is:  every sentence has a subject and a predicate. The predicate contains a verb with a complement or a direct object. A subject
plus a verb without a direct object is described as an intransitive
sentence. A subject with a verb plus a direct object is described as
a transitive sentence. In the inflectional pattern of the Indo-European languages the subject of both of these sentences is in the nominative case and the direct object of the transitive sentence is in the
accusative case.

2.0132 In Basque, traditional analysis requires us to say that
the subject of the transitive sentence is marked by a special inflection, the ergative case. The direct object of a sentence containing an
ergative noun phrase has no case inflection. The subject of the intransitive sentence has the same inflection as the object of the transitive sentence, zero. The easiest course of action for scholars reared
in the European tradition has been to try to explain away the Basque
set-up in the terms of the Indo-European scheme. This was easily accomplished by adopting the passive explanation of the transitive sentence. A transitive sentence with an ergative subject was analyzed

as a passive sentence wherein the ergative inflection was considered
to be the agent complement of a passive verb.  The direct object was
then rescued from its uncomfortable role as a direct object.  There
was always one very troublesome fact:  there is no active paraphrase
for this posited passive construction.  This disturbs the unquestioned
or unconscious assumption that the subject-object functional relationship is somehow universal or given.  It is clearly the notion "subject
of" that has caused the most havoc in the discussion of Basque grammar.
The principal question in an Indo-European grammatical analysis is
which noun phrase is to be marked by the nominative case.  This is
answered by finding the subject in a surface analysis.  In Basque this
is both unnecessary and misleading.  However, since every sentence containing a noun phrase in Basque seems to contain a noun phrase marked
with zero or with the pronoun reflex of one, some grammarians by a sort
of perverse logic have designated this noun phrase as nominative.
This led to the odd situation where the noun phrase that would be
labeled accusative in an Indo-European-type grammar is marked nominative in Basque.  At least a part, perhaps the greater part, of the
controversy about the passivity of the Basque verb has been caused by
simple terminological confusion.  This controversy represents one of
the drearier chapters in the history of grammatical studies.  The hunt
for subject and object in the specific terms of a nominative-accusa-
tive-type grammar could and did lead only to perplexity, for the terms
of traditional grammar simply do not apply to Basque.

2.0133  The application of the technical vocabulary of grammar
thus did not correspond to the correct intuitions of the grammarians
and of the native speakers.  This accounts for the downright arbitrary
character of most immediate constituent analyses.  As it turns out,
the results of most immediate constituent analyses are correct, but
not for the purported reasons.  The constituents of a sentence are not
to be uncovered by a series of successive splits where "sentence"
breaks down into "noun phrase" plus "verb phrase" and then "verb
phrase" breaks down into "noun phrase" plus "verb" and so on.  No
matter how each successive split is labeled and elaborated, the result

will be unsatisfactory in some degree.  A phrase structure grammar
derived in this manner is not only awkward in the extreme, but it also
contradicts reality.

2.014  It is evident from the arguments above that the transformational model of grammar unmodified is not adequate for explaining the
data.  I submit that a model with a base generated in the fashion indicated by the speculations of Fillmore's very influential *case grammar*
offers us a tool for approaching these problems, which will be satisfactory for the provisional treatment of problems in this section.  The
major modification to TG provided by this model will be that it holds
that the relationships between NP and V have semantic content and that
assignments of the functions, subject-of or object-of, are secondary,
not primary as in PS grammar.  Paul Postal (1971:3-4) describes the
situation rather dramatically:

My position is that serious grammatical investigation at
the moment is rather like traveling in quicksand.  There are
no firm supports.  Every step is uncertain.  Every move is
questionable.  There are no well worked out, unshakable
analyses of particular portions of individual languages from
which general principles of grammar can be inferred.  There
are few well-supported, substantively detailed general principles of grammar that can serve as a guide in the analysis
of particular cases.  The linguist interested in providing
a principled account of a significant range of actual factual
details must thus stumble around trying to formulate a general principle here or there that can constrain the description of a particular facts and trying to find firm analyses
of factual fragments that will constrain the formulation of
universal linguistic principles.  Ill-considered boasts to
the contrary, *we are*, in short, *really almost at the beginning of the study of the incredibly complex and still largely
unknown domain of natural language grammar*.  [emphasis mine]
This state of affairs is at once exasperating and stimulating.  It is
exasperating because too much ink is being expended upon abstruse

theoretical quibbles that are as sterile and dessicated as any late
scholastic debate.

2.015 Fillmore's notion of deep case--in contrast to surface
case--permits us to label the functions of noun phrases within a sentence and to establish a hierarchy of those functions. His theory
received its best-known exposition in the now famous essay, "The case
for case" (1968). Fillmore's signal claim is "that a designated set
of case categories is provided for every language with more or less
specific syntactic, lexical, and semantic consequences, and that the
attempt to restrict the notion of 'case' to the surface structure must
fail" (1968:20). The radical proposal is that the relationship between
any noun phrase and the verb is a labeled "semantic" function. This
labeled function is the deep case. Stated more fully and in other
words, there is one verb for every simplex sentence and one or more
noun phrases may be "predicated" of this verb. A sentence is then a
systematic conglomeration of "predicates" attached to the verb. The
number and type of noun phrases that can be attached is determined by
the verb itself. The relationships expressed by these statements might
be diagrammed in the following fashion:

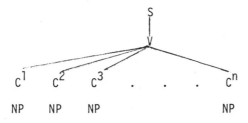

Figure 7

where every C represents a deep case. Fillmore proposes that each case
relationship can occur only once in a given simplex sentence. More
than one occurrence of a single case relationship will point to a complex sentence. Each individual verb then will permit only a limited
number of case relationships. These case relationships are also limited

in number, but not yet exhaustively catalogued.

2.016 I would like to contrast the kind of analysis employed in the diagrams above with what this theory would suggest. Let us examine the following sentence from our text:

9. *etzuen batere erran bere anderari galdu zituela mandoak.*

He did not even tell his wife that he had lost the mules.

For the convenience of the reader I shall supply a preliminary incomplete morpheme by morpheme explication of the surface form of the sentence with a short explanation of some rather simple phonemic alternations that occur in it.

9a.

| EZ+ZU+EN | BATERE | ERRAN | BERE | ANDERE+AR+I |
|---|---|---|---|---|
| not+he has it+PAST | even | told | his own | wife+the+to |

| GALDU | ZITU+EN+LA | MANDO+AK |
|---|---|---|
| lost | he has them+PAST+that | mule+PLURAL+the |

There are simple late phonological rules that make the conversions: *ez+zuen → etzuen* and *zituen+la → zituela*. The mode of derivation is shown in Figures 8, 9, and 10. Loosely ordered the transformational steps that convert the base phrase marker (Fig. 8) into the surface realization of the sentence (Fig. 10) are:

a. optional PRO-deletion
b. *la*-extraposition
c. Negative auxiliary fronting
d. Optional noun phrase displacement in *la*-clause.

We are confronted with some major difficulties in a configurational analysis of the sentence. There are two NP's in the VP. One of these is affixed with the ergative postposition -$k$ and the other with the dative postposition -$i$. We find more than a little difficulty in assigning these postpositions on the basis of this phrase marker. This difficulty is illustrated even more pointedly by the following sentence.

10. *famak kurritu zuen zer nahi diru galdu zutela.*

The rumor was going about that they lost a great deal of money. The difficulties are shown in a tree diagram, Figure 11. This is quite unsatisfactory because it leaves us with an empty node in the diagram.

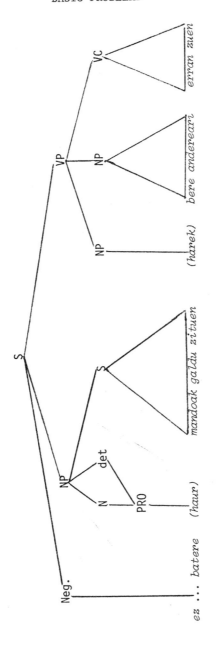

Figure 8

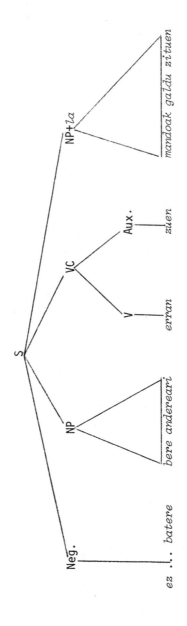

Figure 9

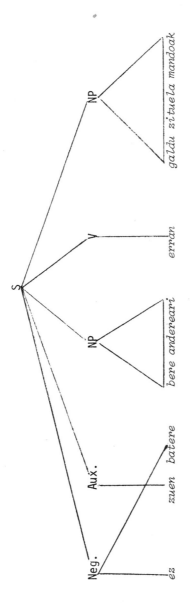

Figure 10

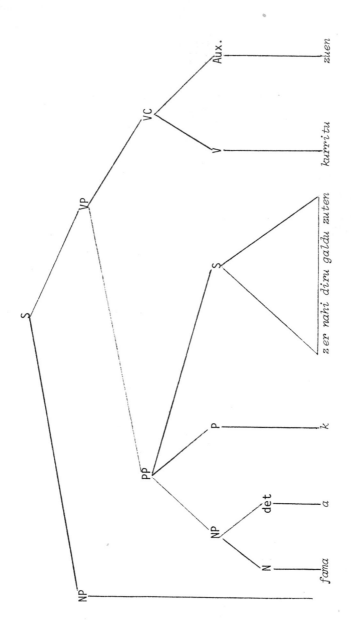

Figure 11

There is no neutral subject.  Insertion of *hura* in this empty node
would yield nonsense.  We certainly cannot explain away this configuration by accepting Lafon's statement (1943:23 *et passim*) where he describes such verbs as *kurritu* as having an "indice de 3$^e$ pers. ne dé-
signant aucun objet précis."  This would not permit us to treat the
obvious exception feature in an acceptable manner.  If the sentence is
diagrammed in the alternate subject-predicate conception, the results
are equally unsatisfying; see Figure 12.  Since *-k* would presumably be
assigned to the subject NP on the basis of a NP in the VP without a
postposition, it would be equally difficult to explain this sentence
and the following two sentences.

11. *hurak kurritzen du.*

    The water is running.

12. *aise kurritzen du.*

    He runs with ease.

However we do find the following:

13. *hiri guzia kurritu dut.*

    I have walked through the whole village.

This offends us because *kurritu* is by all rights and according to tradition an intransitive verb.  To sum it up, we can say that a systematic breakdown of a sentence according to a phrase structure grammar
that yields a configurational analysis depends for its correct interpretation more upon our good will than upon any lucid or explanatory
insights into the sentence.

   2.017  If we approach the analysis of sentence 9 from the point
of view that Fillmore suggests, we might draw a tree diagram with provisional labels as follows in Figure 13.  The labels of this tree are
quite different.  It must be taken into account that the verb *erran* has
a specific content "to tell, to say."  This is a verb whose content,
which is based upon our experience of the real world, must require an
animate human agent for its performance.  Somebody has to tell something to someone.  The verb is necessarily accompanied by two NP's
that stand in an object relationship to it:  a personal one, the person

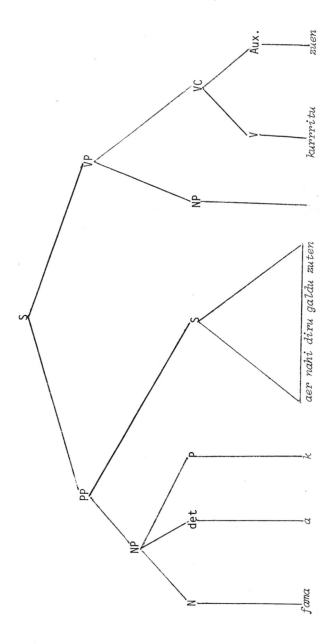

Figure 12

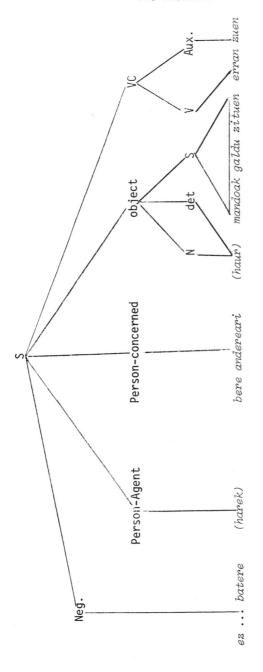

Figure 13

to whom the locutionary act is directed, and an inanimate one, that
one that represents the content conveyed by that locutionary act.  This
rather awkward paraphrase of the grammatical content of sentence 9
states in a rather vague and impressionistic way the labeled relationships that are repeated over and over again in every sentence of any
language.  However, the constellation of these relationships varies
from simplex sentence to simplex sentence, i.e. from verb to verb.  It
will be the burden of my argument that these labeled relationships are
given in deep structure.  There is not necessarily a one for one relationship between deep structure case relationships and surface case
forms.  Sometimes the path from the former to the latter is rather
devious, for frequently some adjustments have to be made.  I shall en-
deavor to demonstrate in a practical way that the results are quite
satisfactory, for the base component of a grammar composed in this
manner makes statements about how real relationships are realized in
linguistic roles.  The base tells us something about the manner in
which the human being arranges his cognitions linguistically.  Any such
statements, however, say nothing about the psychological formation of
these cognitions and nothing about the genetic origin of this arrangement of cognitive elements.  In short, no judgments are made about how
judgments are formed.  An extensive discussion of such great questions,
the importance of which I would not for a moment deny, would carry our
discussion into realms of epistemology and metaphysics from which we
might not safely return.  It is a truism to say that we are all born
with metaphysical prejudices.  It is our task to clarify those prejudices, not to hide them under other more recondite assumptions.  Charles
Fillmore's thesis is in the current jargon "intuitively attractive."
Fillmore calls judgments about the relationships between verbs and
their associated noun phrases *roles* and says (1968:15):

> In particular, I believe that these role types can be identified
> with certain quite elementary judgments about the things that to
> on around us:  judgments about who does something, who experiences
> something, who benefits from something, where something happens,

what it is that changes, what it is that moves, where it starts
out, and where it ends up. Such judgments like these are very
much like the kinds of things grammarians have associated for
centuries with the uses of grammatical "cases," I have been re-
ferring to these roles as case relationships, or, simply, cases.
He explains later on that a grammar is characterized by a "fixed number of role types." The latter observation is also in accord with
traditional grammatical observations. Since the range of human experience, and the measure of it, is almost unlimited, we can adequately
account for the fact that we often find linguistically framed cognition
inadequate to the feeling about the content of that cognition. This
is the eternal complaint of the poet. It lies in the nature of the
linguistic mechanism that there is often a discrepancy between the
psychological reality of a situation and its linguistic expression. A
linguistically adept person can and does by his more skillful use of
these limited means overcome apparent limitations to linguistic expression. This is a matter of superior performance. It behooves us,
then, to show how language does express what it does express in situa-
tions that demand only adequacy to the purpose. The kind of linguistic expression that lies between adequate and superior is grist for
the mills of the literary critic.

2.018 A simple illustration of a possible interpretation according to the parameters of CG can be shown in sentence 9: an animate
human performer engaged in an act of locution that conveyed a certain
content and this act was direct to and experienced by another human
being. This little scenario is concentrated in a verb frame [*erran*
A O D] or in extended terms [*erran* A O E].[9] In the case of other acts
(functions, predications) the number of noun phrases and their potential
relationships with the verb will be different, for other verbs presumably have different real contents. We must conclude that the human
being is wired to classify the infinite multiplicity of real relationships into a limited number of classes of relationships, all the members
of which share some degree of resemblance. One might go a step further

and speculate that they are perceived as such, limiting necessarily the
number of classes of linguistically expressible relationships, and making of deep cases the ultimate terms of sentence formulation. It follows that surface assignment of subject-of, object-of functions are
secondary. Fillmore developed the practical consequence of this notion
in *The Case for Case* when he proposed that all noun phrases in sentences
are provided with adpositions (prepositions, postpositions), requiring,
therefore, that subjectivization and objectivization involve simple deletion as well as surface-positioning. This brought surface structure
closer to the posited deep structure. In the case of Basque we might
guess that ergatives are underlying subjects for which Basque grammar
provides no postposition-deletion rule. As a matter of fact this
assumption, attractive as it seems, only complicates the grammar in that
subjects of intransitive verbs would be unaccounted for. Fillmore aban-
doned the position for a very similar reason, using the example of the
English passive agent *by* (1977:64-65). Adposition insertion near surface realization is the more efficient assumption. This point of view
leads us to the notion that assignment of subject-of, object-of, indi-
rect-object-of functions is a surface device, one that makes the assignment on independent grounds.

2.019  In order to lay a proper foundation for the acceptance or
rejection of the theory described above, we must test the two sets of
notions, the deep cases and the surface cases, against each other on the
facts of Basque sentences. Only examination of the surface categories,
established by a long tradition of grammar, can determine the descriptive adequacy of the proposed deep cases and resolve the all too apparent discrepancy between the two levels. First of all, we may define
for Basque surface grammar four *syntactic* cases: *ergative, neutral,
dative,* and *allocutive*. These are language-specific distinctions that
are to be justified by the fact that pronominal reflexes of the noun
phrases labeled thus in the sentence are obligatorily placed in the
finite verb forms. The *partitive* case can be treated as a conditioned
variant of neutral in that its occurrence depends upon a set of factors

including negation and definiteness.  Allocutive is seldom realized as
a noun phrase except in those cases where the finite form of the verb is
deleted.  The additional postpositional cases, *inessive, allative, abla-
tive,* etc., can be described as lexical cases inasmuch as they have
readily identifiable semantic content.  This distinction will undergo
fairly extensive elaboration, for it appears that these latter cases are
introduced into the sentence structure under the *locative* node, perhaps
by a set of special verbs.  This peculiar observation more than any
other supports their characterization as lexical cases, for it may turn
out that they have sentential origin.  The lexical cases are accordingly
not represented by pronoun reflexes in the finite verb forms, which
would stress their adventitious nature.  The cases initially posited by
Fillmore (1968:24-25) were characterized as follows:

The cases that appear to be needed include:

*Agentive* (A), the case of the typically animate perceived instigator of the action identified by the verb.

*Instrumental* (I), the case of the inanimate force or object
causally involved in the action or state identified by the verb.

*Dative* (D), the case of the animate being affected by the state
or action identified by the verb.

*Factitive* (F), the case of the object or being resulting from
the action or state identified by the verb, or understood as part
of the meaning of the verb.

*Locative* (L), the case which identified the location or spatial
orientation of the state or action identified by the verb.

*Objective* (O), the semantically most neutral case, the case of
anything representable by a noun whose role in the action or state
identified by the verb is identified by the semantic interpretation
of the verb itself; conceivably the concept should be limited to
things which are affected by the action or state identified by the
verb.  The term is not to be confused with the notion of direct
object, nor with the name of the surface case synonymous with accusative.

This was clearly not intended to be an exhaustive list, for Fillmore
states, "Additional cases will certainly be needed." Indeed, three more
cases were soon added, *Experiencer, Source, Goal* (Cook 1972:35-49).
Martin (1972) succumbed to the perils of too great expansion by positing
at least nine more deep cases. It is all too easy to confuse relationships with lexical categories. Therefore, I adhere to the original list
and to a rigid distinction between syntactic and lexical cases.

2.020   Basque is all too often presented as a language of the type
that possesses an elaborate, even baroque, inflectional, paradigmatic
system, a full nominal declension--with a variable number of cases,
depending upon the preconceptions of the grammarian counting them--
along with a positively labyrinthine verbal conjugation. This is not
so. We might characterize this as the inflectional delusion fostered
by the Latin tradition of composing grammars. The inflectional delusion has given rise to a perfectly monstrous term in Basque grammars,
*superdeclension*. The latter term aims in a clumsy manner at describing the multiplication of elements affixed to a nominal stem, for,
from the inflectional point of view, it would seem that, quite unnatur-
ally, one case form is "inflected" by one more case form or perhaps
two or three. This is all based upon the mistaken notion that Basque
has a look-up inflectional grammar like Greek or Latin. Case grammar
offers the means to remedy the pernicious effects of this illusion. If
we look at any of the standard treatments of Basque grammar, we find a
section devoted to the declension of the noun in the manner of a Latin
grammar. Lafitte (1963:58) indicates the full declension of nouns,
common nouns, in Figure 14. This is a typical paradigm inasmuch as it
systematically arranges in a convenient, but not necessarily internally
motivated, manner the possible combinations of nouns with determinants
and postpositions. It represents, in short, a handy checklist. However,
the paradigmatic arrangement does not and cannot explain how this arrangement of items within the Noun Phrase came about. It provides us
with the illusion that these possible sequences are the primary segments of the sentence that are combined at will with other members of

Declension of Common Nouns

(*buru* "head"; *gain* "top")

| Case | Indefinite | | Definite | | Plural |
|---|---|---|---|---|---|
| | Vocalic Stem | Consonantal Stem | Vocalic Stem | Consonantal Stem | All Stems |
| Neutral | *buru* | *gain* | *buru-A* | *gain-A* | *buru-ak* |
| Ergative | *buru-k* | *gain-E-k* | *buru-A-k* | *gain-A-k* | *buru-E-k* |
| Instrumental | *buru-z* | *gain-E-z* | *buru-A-z* | *gain-A-z* | *buru-E(TA)-z* |
| Inessive | *buru-TA-n* | *gain-E-TA-n* | *buru-A-n* | *gain-E-A-n* | *buru-E-TA-n* |
| Elative | *buru-TA-rik* | *gain-E-TA-rik* | *buru-tik* | *gain-E-tik* | *buru-E-TA-rik* |
| Allative | *buru-TA-rat* | *gain-E-TA-rat* | *buru-rat* | *gain-E-rat* | *buru-E-TA-rat* |
| Locative Genitive | *buru-TA-ko* | *gain-E-TA-ko* | *buru-ko* | *gain-E-ko* | *buru-E-TA-ko* |
| Possessive Genitive | *buru-r-en* | *gain-en* | *buru-A-r-en* | *gain-A-r-en* | *buru-E-n* |
| Dative | *buru-r-i* | *gain-i* | *buru-A-r-i* | *gain-A-r-i* | *buru-E-i*   *buru-e-r* |
| Comitative | *buru-r-ekin* | *gain-ekin* | *buru-A-r-ekin* | *gain-A-r-ekin* | *buru-E-ekin* |
| Partitive | *buru-r-ik* | *gain-ik* | Note the article *a* and the *e* in the inessive of *gain*. | | Note *ta* in the locative cases and the *e* of the plural. |
| Prolative | *buru-tzat* | *gain-tzat* | | | |

Figure 14

the nominal class and, further, with members of the more complex verbal
paradigms.  In other words, the illusion consists of the notion that
the members of these paradigms are the primitive terms in the system.
Those terms bear such descriptions as:

> Nominative
> Definite
> Plural

No one can deny the usefulness of such paradigms as an initial descriptive device.  However, we must note that the apparently cross-classified
labels [Nominative], [Definite], [Plural] are not all of the same
nature.  In fact, they do not admit of cross-classification.  A superficial examination of the Basque paradigm will reveal that the elements
as named seem to come in the order:  *Noun - Definite - Plural - Nominative*, for the morphemes representing each parameter are rather easy to
identify.  This would indicate that the modifying elements are introduced in some sort of order.  The systematic information provided by
the paradigm turns out to be morphophonemic rather than grammatical,
for it tells the adjustments to phonemic shapes that automatically take
place in the noun phrase.  The grammatical information provided by the
surface form of the noun phrase only serves as the starting point for
the investigation of deeper relationships.  The noun phrase represents
the endpoint of a derivation rather than its beginning.  In a very
strict sense a paradigmatic analysis of the sentence leads to an artificial segmentation of the sentence.  While the surface analysis of a
sentence seems concrete and easily subjected to analysis, there is
always the very real intuition that functions and relationships that
are active in the physiology of the sentence are somehow disguised by
the surface form.

2.021  Thus far we have determined the constituents of the sentence to be S, PP, NP, VP, VC, V, AUX, ADV.  The definitions have been
ostensive.  We have also observed that the constituent NP can dominate
another constituent PRO.  The immediate object of our attention is the
NP and the PP that dominates it, for we must attempt to determine the

actual content of the members of the traditional paradigm.  In so doing,
we must search out the processes whereby the surface case form, represented by a postposition in all cases save one is assigned.  According
to the terms of case grammar there are a limited number of deep or
underlying relationships, i.e. deep cases, that may be variously represented on the surface.  The syntax of the NP and its dominating PP is
concerned first and foremost with the manner in which and the place
where the surface case is assigned.  All other things follow from this.
Let us examine some sentences.

14. *mandozain batek irabazi zuen parioa.*

    One mule-driver won the bet.

15. *arropa beltz ederrenak ezerten dituzte.*

    They put on the most beautiful black dresses.

The constituents of the noun phrases are sufficiently different to allow us a rather broad discussion.  A deep structure analysis of the
sentences can be diagrammed, as in Figures 15 and 16.

    2.022  In the noun phrase *mandozain batek*, the *-ek* is the post-
position that indicates the ergative case or function.  Some grammarians call this a case-ending.  As will become evident in the course of
the examination of our Basque sentences, the so-called case-endings act
more like the prepositions of the modern Romance and Germanic languages
of Europe.  Unlike the inflectional case-endings of the older Indo-
European languages that govern a single noun or adjective and that are
repeated when noun and adjective are in the same noun phrase, the
Basque postpositions govern the entire NP.  Therefore, it is convenient
in our derivations to set up a node PP that dominates NP in order to
express the relationships that subsist in NP + P.  Since the postposition follows the noun phrase, it is apt to call it a postposition.  In
general in Basque the  distinction between singular and plural is
signaled by different sequences of surface morphemes.  This particular
postposition belongs to a very short list of exceptions.  It is one of
the very few portmanteau morphemes in the Basque nominal system.  *ek*
contains at least three constituents:  ergative, singular, and indef-

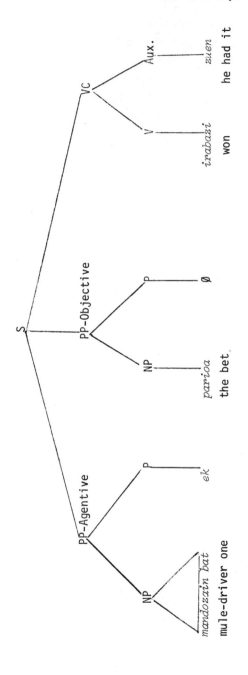

Figure 15

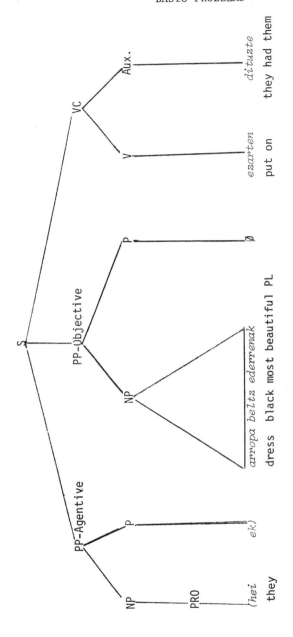

Figure 16

inite. These parameters represent three different categories: surface
case, number, and determination. In this particular case, the terms
singular and indefinite are automatic and predictable since the postposition is suffixed to a numeral *bat* "one." The numeral *bat* also
operates as the equivalent of the indefinite article of English and the
Romance languages. In an isolated sentence,

16. *mandozainbat ikusi dut*

it would be automatically interpreted as an indefinite article. Thus
the translation of the sentence would be "I saw a mule-driver," rather
than "I saw one mule-driver." The choice of interpretation between
"one" and "a," i.e. interpretation as a numeral or as a kind of determination, seems to depend upon the fact that sentence 16 is isolated
or initial in a discourse while in the case of sentence 14 the notion
of more than one mule-driver has been introduced by a previous sentence
in the discourse. The interpretation "one" is accompanied by an im-
plied negative "one mule-driver and not two (or three) mule-drivers,"
whereas "a" is merely an introductory existential assertion. It is of
importance to note that in the next sentence of a potential discourse
following sentence 16 *mandozain* both in Basque and English must occur
with the definite article, Basque *-a*, *-ak* in the ergative:

17. *eta mandozainak ikusi nu.*

  and the mule-driver saw me.

The particular use of the numeral *bat* in sentence 16 might be called
the "discourse-introductory" article. Despite common usage, it is in
no sense "indefinite." Syntactically the form has switched categories
from *numeral* to *determinant*. This switch comes about only when a new
topic in the form of a noun is introduced into a sequence of thought-
connected sentences. This sequence makes up a unit of linguistic substance longer than a sentence. We might call it, for want of a more
exact term, a *paragraph*. The sentences in this unit are interconnected
by suprasentential syntactic and semantic linkages. Linkages of this
nature have received too little attention in linguistic study. They
may furnish us with important clues for a more satisfactory manner of

treating certain classes of conjunctive adverbs such as adversatives. In sentence 17 we must note that the definite article occurs in the form $a$ to which is suffixed $k$, the postposition indicating the ergative case.

2.023 At this point we must take into account one very striking idiosyncracy in the numeral system of Basque. While the numeral *bat* follows the N in the NP, all other numerals immediately precede the N. In sentence 1 we note *bi mandozain basiren*. This holds true for all numerals higher than one, *bi* "two," *hiru(r)* "three," *lau(r)* "four" (see Fig. 17). This seemingly anomaly is not so surprising when we keep in mind the dual syntactic role of *bat*.

### A LIST OF BASQUE NUMERALS

| | | | |
|---|---|---|---|
| 1 | *bat* | 21 | *hogoi-ta-bat* |
| 2 | *bi, biga* | 30 | *hogoi-ta-hamar* |
| 3 | *hiru(r)* | 39 | *hogoi-ta-hemeretzi* |
| 4 | *lau(r)* | 40 | *berrogoi, berhogoi* |
| 5 | *bortz* | 50 | *berrogoi-ta-hamar* |
| 6 | *sei* | 60 | *hirur-hogoi* |
| 7 | *zazpi* | 70 | *hirur-hogoi-ta-hamar* |
| 8 | *zortzi* | 80 | *laur-hogoi* |
| 9 | *bederatzi* | 90 | *laur-hogoi-ta-hamar* |
| 10 | *hamar(r)* | 100 | *ehun* |
| 11 | *hameka* | 200 | *berrehun* |
| 12 | *hamabi* | 300 | *hirur-ehun* |
| 13 | *hamahiru(r)* | 400 | *laur-ehun* |
| 14 | *hamalau(r)* | 500 | *bortz-ehun* |
| 15 | *hamabortz* | 600 | *sei-ehun* |
| 16 | *hamasei* | 700 | *zazpi-ehun* |
| 17 | *hamazazpi* | 800 | *zortzi-ehun* |
| 18 | *hemezortzi* | 900 | *bederatzi-ehun* |
| 19 | *hemeretzi* | 1,000 | *mil, mila* |
| 20 | *hogoi* | 1,000,000 | *miliun* |

Figure 17

The forms *biga, mila* occur when the numeral is used independently.

2.024  This introduces an opposition within the category determination, *definite* as opposed to *indefinite*.  It is sometimes difficult to distinguish between *plural* and *indefinite*.  (It is here that we see very clearly the muddiness of the concept of plurality.)  Within the category *determination* we find besides *definite* and *indefinite*, another opposition, *demonstrative* against *non-demonstrative*.  We can substitute for the definite non-demonstrative *a*, the *definite demonstratives: haur(r), hori, hura*.  In sentence 17, for instance, *mandozain* with demonstrative plus ergative postposition would read *mandozain hunek ikusi nu* "this mule-driver saw me"; *mandozain horrek* ... "that mule-driver ..."; *mandozain harek* ... "that mule-driver over there or out of sight."  This shows that Basque has a demonstrative of three degrees of demonstration.  Henceforth I shall refer to these as demonstratives of the first, second, third degree, respectively (see Fig. 18).

## Demonstratives

| First Degree | *haur* | Singular |
|---|---|---|
| Neutral | | *haur* |
| Ergative | | *hun-ek* |
| Instrumental | | *hun-ta-z* |
| Inessive | | *hun-ta-n* |
| Elative | | *hun-ta-rik* |
| Allative | | *hun-ta-rat* |
| Locative genitive | | *hun-ta-ko* |
| Possessive genitive | | *hun-en* |
| Dative | | *hun-i* |
| Comitative | | *hun-ekin* |

| First Degree | *haur* | Plural |
|---|---|---|
| Neutral | | *hauk* |
| Ergative | | *haui-ek* |
| Instrumental | | *haui-e-ta-z* |
| Inessive | | *haui-e-ta-n* |
| Elative | | *haui-e-ta-rik* |
| Allative | | *haui-e-ta-rat* |
| Locative genitive | | *haui-e-ta-ko* |
| Possessive genitive | | *haui-en* |
| Dative | | *haui-e-ri* |
| Comitative | | *haui-ekin* |

| Second Degree | *hori* | Singular |
|---|---|---|
| Neutral | | *hori* |
| Ergative | | *horr-ek* |
| Instrumental | | *hor-ta-z* |
| Inessive | | *hor-ta-n* |
| Elative | | *hor-ta-rik* |
| Allative | | *hor-ta-rat* |

Figure 18 (cont'd)

Figure 18 (cont'd)

[Second Degree     *hori*     Singular]
Locative genitive          *hor-ta-ko*
Possessive genitive        *horr-en*
Dative                     *horr-i*
Comitative                 *horr-ekin*

Second Degree     *hori*     Plural
Neutral                    *hoik*
Ergative                   *hoi-ek*
Instrumental               *hoi-ta-z, hoi-eta-z*
Inessive                   *hoi-ta-n, hoi-eta-n*
Elative                    *hoi-ta-rik, hoi-eta-rik*
Allative                   *hoi-ta-rat, hoi-eta-rat*
Locative genitive          *hoi-ta-ko, hoi-eta-ko*
Possessive genitive        *hoi-en*
Dative                     *hoi-e-ri*
Comitative                 *hoi-ekin*

Third Degree     *hura*     Singular
Neutral                    *hura*
Ergative                   *har-ek*
Instrumental               *har-ta-z*
Inessive                   *har-ta-n*
Elative                    *har-ta-rik*
Allative                   *har-ta-rat*
Locative genitive          *har-ta-ko*
Possessive genitive        *har-en*
Dative                     *har-i*
Comitative                 *har-ekin*

Third Degree     *hura*     Plural
Neutral                    *hek*
Ergative                   *hei-ek*

Figure 18 (cont'd)

| [Third Degree | *hura* | Plural] |
|---|---|---|
| Instrumental | | *hei-e-ta-z* |
| Inessive | | *hei-e-ta-n* |
| Elative | | *hei-e-ta-rik* |
| Allative | | *hei-e-ta-rat* |
| Locative genitive | | *hei-e-ta-ko* |
| Possessive genitive | | *hei-en* |
| Dative | | *hei-er* |
| Comitative | | *hei-ekin* |

(Lafitte, *Grammaire basque*, pp. 82-83)

2.025   It is evident that in the NP we have three constituents
that govern three categories: Noun, Determinant, Numeral.  Each of
these categories has its own internal structure.  And each behaves in
a different syntactic manner.  When·at any point in the determination
of constituents we must introduce a set of features, a complex symbol,
we have in effect defined a *category*.  Determinant is a good example
of this.  We find that the necessary way of treating any constituent
in this position is to resolve it into features that can be cross-
classified.  We see that a rough approximation of the features of this
category are *definite : indefinite; demonstrative : non-demonstrative;
near : far,* where the features *near : far* are redundantly absent in
the case of a non-demonstrative.  We can propose a tentative cross-
classification of features for the determinants discussed thus far:

*bat*    [-definite, -demonstrative]
*a*      [+definite, -demonstrative]
*haur*   [+definite, +demonstrative, +near, -far]
*hori*   [+definite, +demonstrative, -near, -far]
*hura*   [+definite, +demonstrative, - near, +far]

The three-way split in the demonstrative may well turn out to correspond to the three-way split in the personal pronoun system.  It must

be noted that we have in fact arrived at the constituent N up to this
point by elimination.  The NP's examined up to this point have the
following structure, see Figure 19.

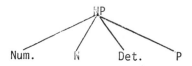

Figure 19

When the numeral is *bat*, this tree takes the form as in Figure 20.

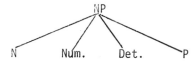

Figure 20

2.026   As we have seen above, under the category *determinant*
there can be inserted a class of lexical items that can be rather
easily analyzed into semantic features that are cross-classified.  In
this position we find, in addition, a very particular postposition,
*-rik*, whose occurrence depends upon the presence of other features,
negation, interrogation or conditional, in the sentence.  In traditional grammars of Basque this is called the *partitive case*.  In contrast to other cases or postpositions, its use is severely restricted,
so much so that I am inclined to remove it from the case system and
treat it as part of the determinant system.[10] Note the following sentences:

18. *ogia dut*

   I have (some) bread.

19. *ez dut ogirik.*

   I haven't any bread.   or    I have no bread.

20. *badea ogirik?*

   Is there any bread?

21. *haren behorrik ikusten baduzu ...*

   If you see any of his mares / any mare of his ...

I shall demonstrate below how a feature analysis, which is more complete than the one suggested above, will simplify the presentation of the partitive function and smoothly account for such sentences as:

22. *liburu batzu badut.*

   I have some books.

In sentence 15 we find two more constituents, both of which belong to what is traditionally referred to as the *adjective*. I shall show that this class of constituents is secondary. That is to say, it has been inserted into the noun phrase transformationally. This fact is to be revealed by some surface commutation that will lead to a deep-structure analysis. Note the following noun phrase from sentence 15:

23. *arropa beltz ederrenak.*

   The most beautiful black dresses.

The surface removal of one element, the *en* of *ederrenak* "the most beautiful (ones)" yields a perfectly well-formed noun phrase:

24. *arropa beltz ederrak.*

   The  beautiful black dresses.

*en* can be interpreted as an affix of degree. In sentence 23 it is a *superlative* affix. Semantically one of the class meanings of the category adjective is *quality* and quality admits of degree. Logically some members of the class adjective admit of no degree. English *unique*, for example, is one of these. The class meaning of the affix permits us to form apparently grammatical, but illogical sentences containing *most unique, not very unique, more unique*. It is this contradiction between semantic content and class operations that permits rhetorical flourishes

such as irony, sarcasm, and just plain sloppy thinking.  A search for
other affixes of this nature in Basque turns up additionally:  *egi*
"excessive," *ago* "comparative," as well as *en* "superlative."  They
yield these modifications of the adjective *eder(r)*:

25. *ederregi*

   too beautiful

26. *ederrago*

   more beautiful

27. *ederren*

   most beautiful

The possibility of modification of these lexical items with this class
of affixes is one of the defining features of the class adjective.  The
shuffling about of elements yields also the following three noun
phrases:

28. *arropa beltzak*

   the black dresses

29. *arropa ederrak*

   the beautiful dresses

30. *arropak*

   the dresses

In this case *ak* combines *a*, the definite article, and *k*, the postposition indicating ergative.  It is important to note that plurality as
well as definiteness modifies the entire noun phrase.  We would add to
the list of features of the determinant [± Plural].  However, *singu-
larity : plurality* and certain cases are reflected in the modifications
to the surface verb where no other noun phrase features are.  It may
turn out to be necessary to set up a tree as in Figure 21.  Surface
relationships would seem to cause us to add an optional category to our
tree, (ADJ).  Since the evidence indicates that we can stack adjectives
between noun and determinant, this addition makes it necessary to add
to our rule a recursive one, perhaps of the form:

$$ADJ \rightarrow ADJ\ (ADJ)$$

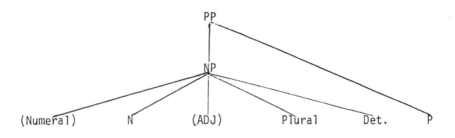

Figure 21

However, this is to be avoided because adjective stacking takes place
in a certain order.
31. *arropa eder beltzak.
This phrase shows us that such a rule would be misleading. Adjective
insertion takes place in quite another fashion. I shall follow the
practice of many recent grammarians and consider adjectives to be
derived immediately from relative clauses and eventually from Verbs.
These posited relative clauses are inserted transformationally into
the noun phrase in a definite order. I suspect that this order is
determined by semantic class. We can consider sentences 28 and 29 to
be derived from the following relative constructions:
32. ederrak diren arropak
    the dresses that are beautiful
33. beltzak diren arropak
    the dresses that are black
The stacking of adjectives is then a kind of ordered conjunctive process as in Figures 22 and 23. The one difficulty to be discussed below
at length is the fact that the noun phrase containing eder(r) cannot
occur to the left of the noun phrase containing beltz. Figure 23 does
not represent the only reduction possible for the tree shown in Figure
22. The following two noun phrases are also accepted by native

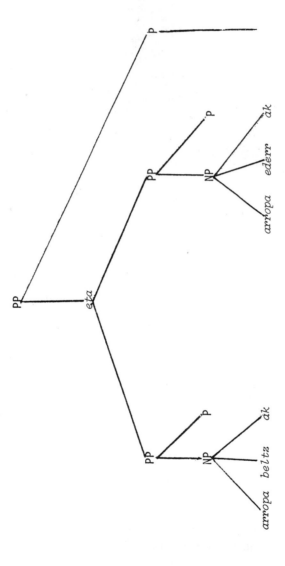

Figure 22

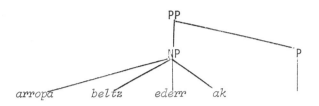

Figure 23

speakers as well-formed.  They represent intermediate steps in the
process of conjunction reduction.

34. *arropa beltzak eta ederrak.*

35. *arropa beltz eta ederrak.*

In order to account for the relative clauses required by the derivation above, we must posit a tree that will account for the sentential
embedding assumed.  A properly constructed tree will be a necessary
aid in the analysis of relative clauses and will also serve to account
for nominal compounding, the genitive in *en*, and the genitive in *ko*.
In the case of the sort of embedding called *relativization* the embedded
sentence must contain a noun phrase that is identical with the noun
phrases directly dominated by PP.  Noun phrases with identical trees
without identical noun phrases are to be treated under *complementation*;
see Figure 24.

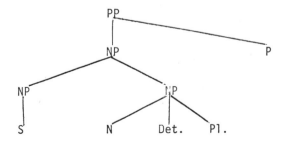

Figure 24

2.027  For the relative clause *beltzak diren arropak*, the following tree can be posited, as in Figure 25:

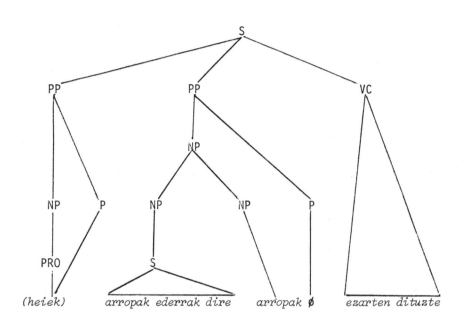

Figure 25

The first transformation to this tree requires these steps:
a. Deletion of the identical NP to the left.
b. Exchange of node S for node NP.  S is pruned.
c. Insertion of *-en*, the relative affix, after the inflected verb.
The process yields a new tree, as in Figure 26.

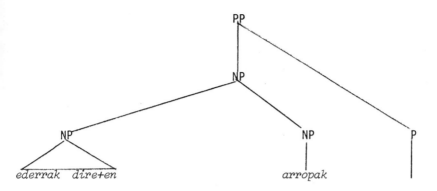

Figure 26

The adjectivization transformation takes place in at least five steps:
a. Erasure of the verb and its affix.
b. Transposition of the left NP to the right.
These steps leave us with an intermediate tree, as in Figure 27.

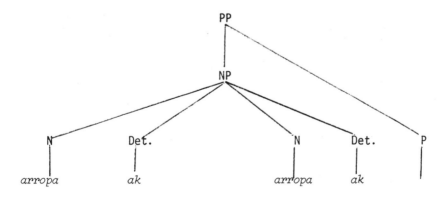

Figure 27

Since the node NP can have only one determinant, the node Det. is erased to the left, yielding the tree in Figure 28.

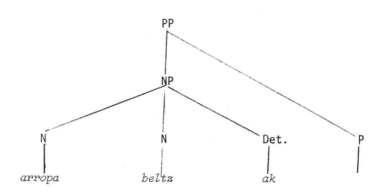

Figure 28

In the short derivations above, it has been expedient to treat determinant and plurality under Det.

The conjunctive transform that will yield *arropa beltz ederrak* can be shown by the following changes to the structure to be found in Figure 22.   The first two steps will yield the tree in Figure 29.
a. Conjoining of two PP's by *eta*.
b. Deletion of one of the identical NP's, in this case to the right.
This yields the noun phrase in sentence 34, *arropa beltzak eta ederrak*.
The second part of the transformation has these steps:
c. Deletion of the two lower PP nodes.
d. Automatic deletion of the node Det. to the left.
This will yield a tree that describes the structure of the noun phrase in sentence 35, *arropa beltz eta ederrak*.   The last step will yield *arropa beltz ederrak*.

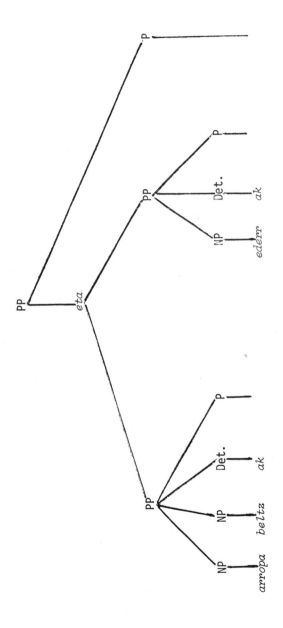

Figure 29

e. Deletion of *eta*.

Placing the adjective directly under the node NP as another NP can be justified by analyzing a sentence that might otherwise appear rather odd.

36. *zuen mutiko espartin beltzak erran daut.*

    Your boy with the black sandals said it to me.

Literally translated the noun phrase would read, "Your black sandal boy." A tree analysis of the entire sentence shows this picture, as in Figure 30. It must be pointed out at this time that in the drawing of this tree the node *adnominal* is an ad hoc invention for two purposes, the immediate analysis of this sentence and an anticipation of the following discussion of the genitive.

     2.028 Although in this particular instance we are only interested in the constituents realized under the node PP, I would like to point out some properties of the Basque sentence. The tree shows us that PP's that dominate PRO's can be, and most often are, deleted when, or rather because, a concord transformation has inserted morphological indications of the proper PRO's under the node V or AUX. In any case sentence 37 is a well-formed sentence in anybody's Basque.

37. *erran daut.*

    He said it to me.

By the deletion operations the original tree can be reduced, as in Figure 31. The PP's labeled *Agentive, Objective,* and *Dative* alone can be deleted in this fashion. The postpositional phrase *muthiko espartin beltz ak* is derived in the same fashion as the adjectives in the previously discussed sentence. It takes place in two steps: (1) relativization, (2) Adjectivization. The matrix sentence is:

38. *muthikoak erran daut.*

    The boy told it to me.

The constituent sentence is:

39. *muthikoak espartin beltzak baditu.*

    The boy has black sandals.

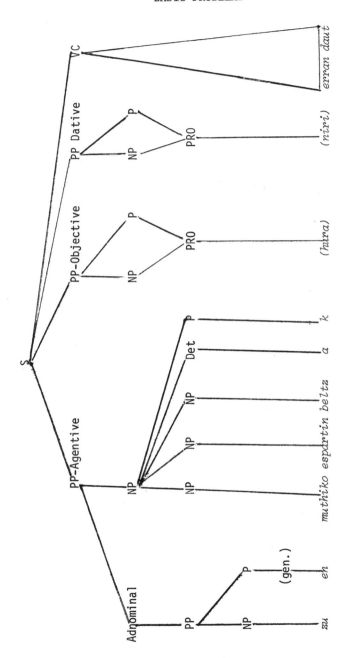

Figure 30

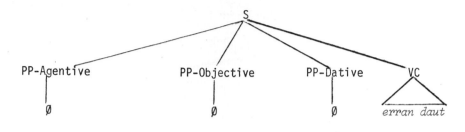

Figure 31

That is to say, it is a case of embedding that might be better stated in this form:

40. *muthikoak [muthikoak espartin beltzak baditu] erran daut.*

This sentence can again be represented as a tree, as in Figure 32.

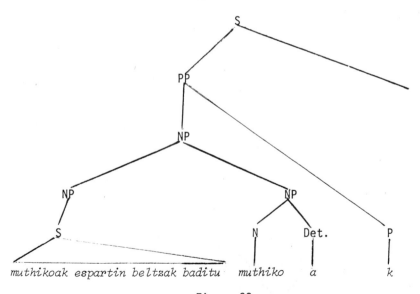

Figure 32

The steps in the derivation of the sentence are:

T-Relativization.

a. Deletion of identical noun.

b. Suffixation of relative suffix to inflected verb.

These operations yield:

41. *espartin beltzak dituen muthikoak* ...

The boy who has black sandals ...

This is a perfectly well-formed PP of the form as in Figure 33.

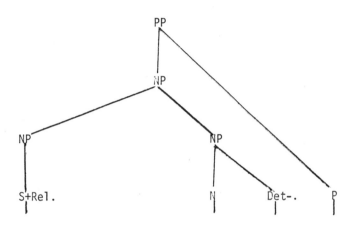

Figure 33

In this structure it is perfectly possible to delete the non-relativized N, yielding a structure as in Figure 34. This yields the noun phrase:

42. *espartin beltzak dituenak.*

This is a perfectly well-formed constituent of a possible sentence:

43. *espartin beltzak dituenak erran daut.*

The one who has black sandals said it to me.

We can now apply the adjectivization transform to the configuration in Figure 34.

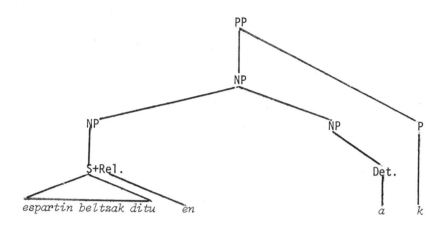

Figure 34


T-Adjectivization
c. Erasure of relativized verb.
d. Transposition of the left NP to the right.
e. Erasure of the node Det. to the left.
This yields:
44. *muthiko espartin beltzak.*

      2.029  The occurrence of an adjective in the noun phrase of a
Basque sentence is, as we have seen, the result of the embedding of a
sentence under the node PP.  We have also seen that a predicate noun
can also appear in the surface representation of a Basque sentence in
the apparent position of an adjective.  The expansion of the application of this series of transformations will take place in the section
on Compound Nouns.  Relativization and Adjectivization are not the only
kinds of embedding.  These two transformations are characterized in the
very first place by the occurrence of identical nouns in the matrix and
constituent sentences.  To sum it all up, the identical noun is erased
in the process of embedding in the constituent sentence while the affix

*en* is suffixed to the inflected verb.  In the next step, all elements
except the predicate of the embedded sentence can be erased and that
predicate is inserted between the N and Det.

Because the obligatory relativization transformations as well as
the optional ones delete a number of formatives, relative constructions
are very often ambiguous in Basque.

45. *ikusi duen gizona.*

This sentence can be interpreted as "the man that he saw" or "the man
who saw him."  Undeleted pronouns in the relative clause will, of
course, remove possible cases of ambiguity.

46. *harek ikusi duen gizona.*

    the man that he saw

47. *hura ikusi duen gizona.*

    the man that saw him

The matter of restrictive as opposed to non-restrictive relative
clauses is rather less troubled than in a language such as English.  In
passing, let us note that for non-restrictive relative clauses Basque
uses apposed clauses with the head N of the apposited relative clause
deleted as in sentence 42.

48. *ikusten zuen ardura bertze mandozaina, bere mandoak ebatsi*
    *zaizkona.*

    He often saw the other mule-driver, who stole his mules from him.

The same sentence with a restrictive clause would read:

49. *ikusten zuen ardura bere mandoak ebatsi zaizkon mandozaina.*

    He often saw the mule-driver that stole his mules from him.

Let us return to the sentence represented in Figure 31.  It has as one
of its constituents the admittedly ad hoc node *adnominal*, as shown in
Figure 35.  It would be hard to overlook the formal resemblance between
the adnominal *zuen muthikoa* and sentence 41, *espartin beltzak dituen*
*muthikoa*.  If a noun plus determinant is substituted for the pronoun,
we find, for example, the noun phrase:

50. *gizonaren muthikoa*

    the man's boy

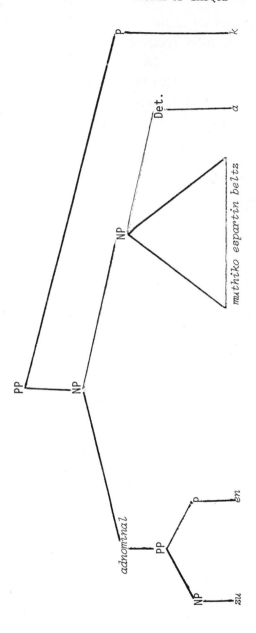

Figure 35

This formal resemblance will lead us to the conclusion that genitive constructions are also embedded sentences. This conclusion, of course, indicates that the *en* of the relative construction is in every respect identical with the postposition *en* of the so-called *possessive genitive*. In terms of simplicity, this is a very attractive proposition. We can diagram sentence 50 in the following fashion, proposing *gizonak muthikoa badu* "the man has the boy" as the relativized S in Figure 36. If we assume a *Genitivizing Transform*, such a transform will delete not only the identical noun but also the verb in the relativized sentence and, in addition, the postposition on the noun that remains, but not the determinative of that noun. As *the* deleted verb in this proposed transform, I shall consistently assume an inflected form of the verb *izan* "to have, to be." This verb is sufficiently vague in its meaning for our immediate purposes. Luckily, the meaning of *izan* in Basque is even vaguer than the meaning of *to have* in English. In Basque it is rather obviously a tense and pronoun-reflex carrier. And, too, it is certainly a seductive notion to derive all *en*-genitive constructions from an underlying sentence containing:

$$[[X \ du \ Y]^S]^{np}$$

If, again, we make a substitution, this time a demonstrative for the definite *a* of *gizon-a-ren*, we find a structure such as in Figure 37. With this tree we can account rather easily for the demonstrative pronouns of the third person. For the third degree pronoun in the diagram can be substituted demonstratives of the first degree, *hun+en* and of the second degree, *horr+en*, with no change to the structure. Pronominalizations in this case seem to be rather simply noun deletions according to the pattern:

*gizon haren muthikoa :: haren muthikoa*

Accounting for the pronouns of the other persons, first and second, the answer will not be so simple. Except for the third person reflexive, for pronouns other than the third person, we find not the affix *en*, but *re*.

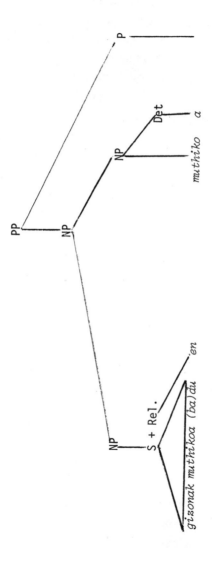

Figure 36

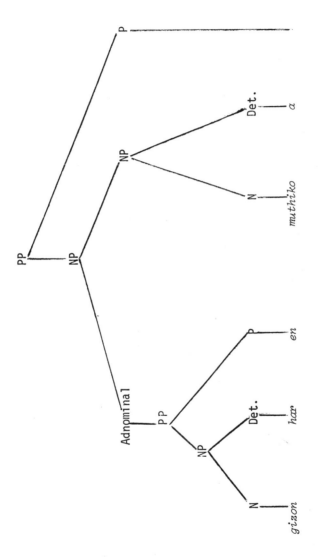

Figure 37

Sg. *ene*   from *\*enre*      my, of me
    *hire*                     your (familiar singular)
    *zure*                     your (polite singular)
    *bere*                     his, her, its, reflexive
Pl. *gure*                     our

We can account for the suffix *re* as being a case of suppletion limited
to a small strictly defined class. We must note that there are two
holes in the paradigm. These are filled with *zuen* "your (polite
plural)" and *beren* "their (reflexive plural)." Owing to the preva-
lence of the contrast *gizonaren* "genitive singular definite" and *gizo-
nen* "genitive indefinite" or "genitive plural definite," there is a
weak feeling that *en* is plural in meaning. This is, however, not
characteristic of the whole Basque system. Examination of the so-
called paradigms of traditional Basque grammars (see above, Fig. 14)
shows that the distinction between singular and plural and the distinction between definite and indefinite are rather difficult to show
paradigmatically. This very feeble singular : plural distinction may
seem to be developed in the form *guren* in a noun phrase:
51. *guren etxea*

   the house of members of our family
The form *guren* does, however, have quite a different derivation. It
is the genitive of *gureak* "our ones." In a very real sense it is a
case of double embedding. It is not related paradigmatically to *gu*
or *gure*. In any case a seemingly superficial aspect of the formal
parallelism between relative clauses and genitive phrases appears to
drop out here. In defense of the term *adnominal* let us examine some
phrases and sentences in which a possessive genitive occurs, and in
which that genitive will not lend itself easily to the analysis of the
*en*-genitive given above. We certainly could not defend at any length
the specious derivation of
52. *gizonaren ama*

the man's mother

from an underlying

53. $[[[gizonak\ ama\ badu]^s\ en]^{rel}\ ama]^{np}$

This would offend us because human kinship relationships are of a
biological nature and are determined solely by the way the world is
put together. The relationship between a man and his mother is not a
matter of possession; it is a limiting relationship inasmuch as it
specifies the relationship of one member to a natural group of which
it is a part. In this case the possession, if it can indeed be described as such, is "inalienable possession." Such relationships,
the relationships within the biological chain, find the parallel in
part-to-whole relationships such as are found in English *the man's
eye, the edge of the sea, the top of the mountain*. It is perhaps better to say that kinship terms belong to a very special class of part-
to-whole relationships. It has some very particular properties of
its own and is far more elaborate in Basque than it is in English.
For the anthropologist and sociologist kinship systems are a rich
source of pertinent information. *gizonaren ama* designates a specific
woman. It is a limiting relationship, not unlike a demonstrative in
its force. The very use of *ama* or any member of its class requires
that somewhere in the discourse this noun must be accompanied by a
delimiting genitive. The occurrence of the genitive is thus lexically
determined. We find the same situation in all part-whole relationships. For instance in

54. *gizonaren begia*

the man's eye

the part-whole relationship is all too evident. A man without an eye
is a victim of misfortune or a freak. Likewise, outside of mythology,
a man without a mother is a total impossibility. The difference between a possessive genitive and the last two delimiting genitives is
that the two latter genitives are unequivocal in that they indicate a
clearly defined relationship within a system, not a conventional system, but a natural system. The relationship in sentence 50, *gizonaren*

*muthikoa,* is quite ill-defined.  The boy may be the man's son, a hired
boy, a boy who lives in his household, or a dozen other possibilities
that can only be narrowed down in the context of an entire discourse
and real situation.  It would seem that a lexical item belonging to
an entity that stands in a real part-to-whole relationship or a kinship relationship belongs to a natural semantic group that carries
with it a feature of determination that turns up on the surface as a
genitive.  In effect, it carries a genitive slot with it, for in real
life a father or a mother is a father or mother of somebody and an eye
is always an essential part of a living being.  It is for such genitives that I reserve the node *adnominal,* a node automatically created
by the presence of certain classes of lexical items.  To sum it up,
there is a class of lexical items such that for each member of that
class there is a feature of determination that specifies its relationship to all other members of that class.  The occurrences of one member of the class demand the co-occurrence of that feature.  For example
in the phrase

55. *etxearen borta*

    the door of the house

*borta* is a feature of a class *etxe*.  The occurrence of *borta* demands
determination.  In the nature of things, a house without a door is an
oddity that demands explanation.  *borta* is not only a feature of the
class *etxe*; it is also a feature of the class *eliza*.  This brings us
to the problem of further defining the nature of class-membership.
And this introduces the genitive in *ko*, the so-called locative genitive.  The underlying relationships in phrases that contain    , for
instance,

56. *etxeko borta*

    the house door

are not so clear as they are in phrases containing *en*.  It is, therefore, very much to the point to examine the grammar of *en-* and *ko-*
genitives at some length.  The burden of this demonstration will be
that Basque treats in a uniform fashion a particular grammatical opera-

tion that other, more familiar languages treat in a variety of ways.
That operation is clearly to be seen in the grammatical behavior and
derivation of the two genitives of Basque, the *en*-genitive and the
*ko*-genitive.

2.030   If we take a look at one of the several standard treatments of the Basque language, all of which are formulated after the
Latin model, we find as two of the entries under nominal declension,
the possessive genitive in *en* and the locative genitive in *ko*.   The
following two noun phrases will illustrate this:

57. *atearen giltza*

  the key of the door

58. *ateko giltza*

  the key of the door

It must be mentioned that the insistence upon the use of the arrangement "nominal declension," according to which nouns are displayed
after the fashion of a Latin grammar, has given rise to a perfectly
monstrous term in Basque grammar, *superdeclension*.   This term aims at
describing the multiplication of elements suffixed to the nominal stem
in a very clumsy fashion.   Since this description is concerned with
showing how one species of this multiplication takes play, it will be
a demonstration of the hopeless inadequacy and deceptiveness of the
inflexional model for the study of Basque.   Its deceptiveness lies in
the fact that it creates the pernicious illusion that Basque has a
sort of look-up grammar like Greek or Latin.   The very naming of the
two genitives, the *possessive genitive* and the *locative genitive,*
does no justice to the grammatical situation, for it merely obfuscates
it.   The term *genitive* puts under one simplifying rubric two end
results of two different and fairly long derivations.   It will be a
salutary gesture to remove from the terminology any mention of *genitives* of any sort.   The term is based upon an erroneous system of
categorial classification.   In so many words, the grammarian is induced to explain the wrong things.   Native grammatical tradition as
well as the extreme discomfort of critical scholars causes us to set

out upon a search for a better description and a more enlightening try
at explanation.

2.031  I would like to examine briefly the unsatisfying results
produced by subscription to the *genitive illusion* in the works of two
well-known scholars of Basque, Antonio Tovar and Nicolás Ormaechea,
also called Orixe.  Tovar tried to discern in the two "genitives" a
contrast between a *determinative* and an *attributive function* (1957:68).
This seductively neat division does point out some grammatical facts
that turn out to be quite incidental.  Tovar is guilty of one venial
and one out-and-out sin.  His error is to treat as the beginning of
analysis and explanation that which is really the final product of a
fairly complex derivation.  His sin was to walk into the taxonomic
booby trap.  He was tricked by a name.  The contrast *determinative-at-
tributive* is empty and trivial.  It belongs to the realm of unnecessary explanations.  If we isolate *atearen giltza* and *ateko giltza*
from their proper sentences, there seems to be a certain amount of
validity in Tovar's classification. We must remind ourselves of the
dangers inherent in the attempt to interpret adequately segments of
syntactic strings that have been arbitrarily isolated from their proper sentences even where--and especially where--that segment seems to
represent an identifiable constituent at one level or another.  When
we do this, we merely provide the reader of our grammar with a kind of
look-up list of possible translations from one language to another
without providing the connecting link, an adequate explanation of how
the translations were, or rather are, to be arrived at.  The term
*locative genitive* is founded upon a very deep intuition.  This posited
intuition is part and parcel of the native oral grammatical tradition,
as Luis Michelena has affirmed in a private communication.  Orixe
(1963:26) is a little more generous to us in his description of the
*ko*-genitive, for he defines it as "The genitive of fixed location, of
where, of when, of time."  The lesser degree of abstraction in this
description provides us with the eventual key for the explication of
the following forms:

59. *mendiko bidea*

     the mountain road, the road in the mountains

60. *menditikako bidea*

     the road from the mountain

61. *mendirako bidea*

     the road to the mountain

62. *\*mendiaren bidea*

     the mountain's road

In his definition of the *en*-genitive Orixe has sneaked in, almost with
the left hand, an *animate-inanimate* distinction, for his description
reads, "Genitive, the genitive of possession of 'who.'" This particular, and not too obvious error finds its origin in the attempt to
find general semantic distinctions in limited surface constructions.
The grammar, because of a number of internal constraints, will not
generate the noun phrase in sentence 62, above. And this is not because *mendi* is not a "who," i.e. a non-animate noun. The attempt to
maintain such an explanation will run up against such common constructions as *mendiaren gainean* "on top of the mountain." The phrases in
sentences 60 and 61 are illustrations of superdeclension. If we interpret such forms from a "declensional" point of view, it appears
that one inflexion has been added to another. To a person soaked in
latinity this would indeed seem to be a sort of perverse oddity. If
the declensional principle were to be carried to its logical conclusion as Orixe seems to want to do in his grammar (1963:24, 30-31),
Basque would have a number of enormously long, and thoroughly unnecessary, nominal paradigms in a very elaborate look-up grammar. If, on
the other hand, we treat these strings of nominal affixes as a sequence
of elements that are systematically added in the course of the generation of Basque sentences, we destroy the inflexional illusion and dis-
miss the offense of superdeclension. In short, we are freed from the
fetters of an inappropriate model. In order to facilitate thie liber-
ation, I shall posit the notion that genitives in *ko*, like the genitives in *en*, represent regularly derived reductions of embedded sen-

tences, which reductions are accomplished when and only when certain
underlying configurations are present and active.  This is a claim
that the noun phrases in sentences 58, *ateko giltza*, and 59, *mendiko
bidea*, represent embeddings of the following sentences:

63a. *giltza atean dago*

    the key is in the door

63b. [[*giltza atean dago*]$^S$ *giltza*]$^{np}$

64a. *bidea mendietan da*

    the road is in the mountains

64b. [[*bidea mendietan da*]$^S$ *bidea*]$^{np}$

In tree diagrams the process can be represented as in Figures 38 and
39.  Within the scope of the matrix sentence, the finite verb is
erased and the noun, to which is affixed the inessive postposition $n$,
is affixed with *ko*.  This is quite clearly a case of noun phrase complementation with the underlying structure, stated in English terms:

    [[The key is in the door] the door]

or in more formal terms:

    [[Det. S] Det.   N]

The formal steps in a posited transformation would be:

  a. Deletion of the identical noun.

  b. Deletion of the verb node in the embedded sentence.

  c. Replacement of the inessive suffix by *ko*.

It is all too evident that *ko* is not an inflexion in the traditional
sense.  It is a noun phrase complementizer and, what is more, a noun
phrase dominated by the *locative* node.  In sentence 60, *menditikako
bidea*, the locative postposition *(e)tik* "from" and in sentence 61,
*mendirako bidea*, the locative postposition *(e)rat* "to, toward" are not
erased from their particular derivations which are certainly identical
to the derivation just traced.  It is just possible that the disappear-
ance of $n$, the inessive postposition, is a fluke of historical phonology.  In fact, I make this claim.

    2.032  To show the difference between a relative embedding and a
complementation embedding, I have taken two quotes from Leiçarraga's

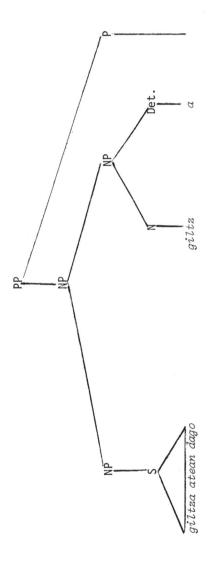

Figure 38

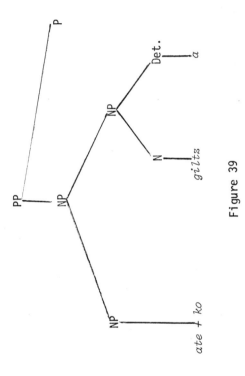

Figure 39

Basque New Testament of 1571 (edited by Linschmann and Schuchardt, 1900).

65. *Iaincoac guregana duen charitatea.*   (John's First Epistle 4:16)
     Charitati quam habet Deus in nobis.

66. *Iaincoaren gureganaco charitatea.*   (John's First Epistle 4:9)
     Charitas Dei in nobis

Again that striking feature of Basque noun phrases whereby *ko* can be suffixed to other locative postpositions is pointed out. This partic- ular feature of Basque morphology remains a bone in the throat of those who wear what Schuchardt called *eine arische Brille* "Indo- European spectacles," This is, of course, the source of the offensive term *superdeclension*. To be sure, this term has its partner in the verbal system, *superconjucation*, see Lafitte (1963:218). Such terms are certain to abound in a description that sees only the continuous addition of new morphemes as a manner of grammatical development. We have seen exactly the same situation in the case of *la* in sentence 9 and in the derivation traced in Figures 8 through 10. It is more than simply a transformationally inserted complement marker; it is a loca- tive postposition with the phonologically determined variations: *la, lat, ra, rat*. It undergoes the same grammatical and syntactic treat- ment as any other locative postposition. Sentence 65 is derived by a relativizing transformation from *Iaincoac charitatea guregana du* em- bedded in a noun phrase headed by *charitatea*, as in Figure 40. The relativization of this structure has two steps:

 a. Deletion of the identical noun in the embedded sentence.

 b. Affixation of the relative affix to the inflected verb.

The genitivation of this structure is accomplished by the further steps of reduction:

 c. Deletion of the inflected verb.

 d. Deletion of the postposition on the NP.

This will yield:

67. *Iaincoaren charitatea*
     God's love

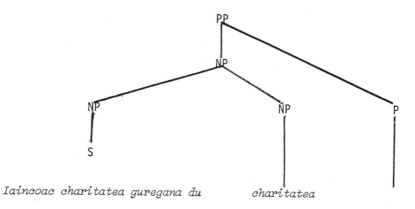

Figure 40

Sentence 66 is curious inasmuch as it seems to contain both relativization and complementation.   In order to account for *gureganako* we must
assume an underlying form, as in Figure 41.

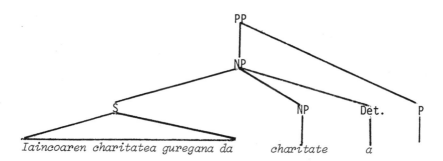

Figure 41

In this particular structure, if we delete all elements except those
dominated by the locative node, *ko* is suffixed to the locative postposition. *ko* does not replace the affix we must assume to be present
in deep structure; it is simply attached to it. A great variety of
postpositions can be inserted under the locative node. They are
semantically unique inasmuch as they describe a unique, but systematically relational locative situation. In this manner they are quite
different from the surface postpositions that indicate directly or indirectly the grammatical relationships of agent, objective, and dative.
The latter are often systematically deleted and replaced in the various transformations. Primarily we must assume that locative postpositions are already present in underlying structures while postpositions for agentive, objective, and dative are assigned later in the
processes that lead to surface realization.

2.033 *la*-complementation is particularly illustrative of this
situation. The following sentences show the systematic affixation of
*ko* very clearly:

68a. *famak kurritu zuen jin zela.*

68b. *jin zelako famak kurritu zuen.*

The rumor of his having come went around.

The configurations are diagrammed in Figures 42 and 43.

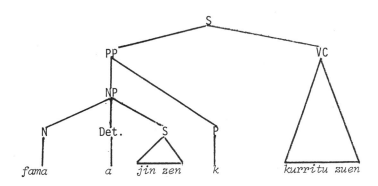

Figure 42

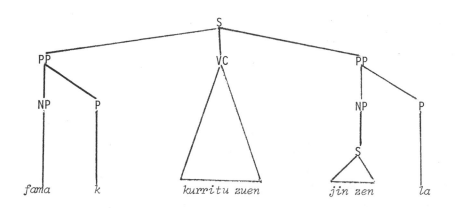

Figure 43

This is the general form of what I have called *la*-complementation. It would be tempting to equate this affix with the English *that*-complementizer. Unfortunately the situation is not that simple. *la*-complementation has some very specific properties that will not permit us to make such an assumption. In the sentence above and in all sentences where *la* .complements occur that complement contains the factual substance of *fama* or any equivalent noun. Note for example in the following two sentences the function of the *la*-complement:

69a. *berria izan duzu loterian irabazi dugula.*
69b. *loterian irabazi dugulako berria duzu izan.*

   You have had the news that we have won in the lottery.
The *la*-complement here *loterian irabazi dugu* "we have won in the lottery" is the factual of *berri* "the news." Lafitte (1963:400) very aptly calls this sort of complementation *le mode des propositions complétives.* I shall adopt his term and refer in the future to *completives.*

   Let us note that the underlying structure of the noun phrase containing such a complement is as follows (Fig. 44):

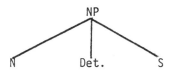

Figure 44

This underlying structure must also be posited where no noun plus
determinant are present in the surface structure. For example, in
sentence 9, *etzuen batere erran bere andereari galdu zutela mandoak,*
there is no head noun in the sentence to correspond to *fama* or *berria.*
It remains because, as a true completive, we must assume a deleted
pronoun in the underlying structure which corresponds in function to
one of those nouns. It is a true completive inasmuch as the *la*-com-
plement contains the substance of what he said. Compare Figure 43.

    2.034 Not all noun phrase complements with the underlying
structure found in Figure 44 are necessarily *la*-complements, that is
to say, true completives. Let us compare the following sentences for
which we must assume a noun phrase structure like that in Figure 44:

70. *nahi duzuea ikhus dezadan nik ere.*

    Do you want me to see her too?

71. *ez dakit ethorriko den.*

    I don't know whether he will come.

72. *badut beldurra oraino ere ogia chuhurtuko den.*

    I am afraid that bread will become scarce again.

73. *nahi dute jaits gaiten.*

    They want us to come down.

74. *manatu du ogia jo zazaten.*

    He has ordered them to thresh the wheat.

The difference between the two kinds of complementation must be the
content of the noun in deep structure that is later deleted. On the

surface the difference is represented by the lack of *la* with the
simultaneous occurrence of a special class of verbal inflexions,
future or subjunctive. According to the scheme presented *hura* represents a noun that is deleted when the constituent sentence, *nik
ikusi dut*, is extraposed. In this latter sentence we might say that
it is a noun with the meaning "wish, desire." Or expressed in terms
of modal logic, a deontic proposition. We might even propose a kind
of cognate construction that would never be realized on the surface:

75. *\*nahia nahi baduzu*

Luckily such a noun is still present in the surface form of sentence
72. That is the noun, *beldurra* "fear." Likewise for sentences 71
and 74, we might propose the following underlying cognate forms:

76. *\*jakintza ez dakit*

77. *\*manamendu manatu du*

In these cases the semantic content of the head noun, present or deleted, represents things or events that remain in unaccomplished
potentiality. Neither "fear," nor "wish," nor "order" represent
realized facts. In order to characterize the underlying structures
that distinguish *la* complements from the latter kind of complement, it
seems necessary to mark the head noun with a semantic feature [$\pm$ Fact].
We can, therefore, refer to noun phrase complements with *la* as *factive
complements*. It would seem at this point that the occurrence of a
prefixing transformation of a *la*-complement with automatic insertion
of *ko* takes place in factive complements. This is to be seen in sentences 68b and 69b, above. Since there is no difference in underlying
configuration between factive and non-factive complements, I have
tried to find an answer in the content of the sentence, specifically,
in the content of the head noun of the complement structure. *ez dakit*
"I don't know" is unrealized knowledge or, at least, something that is
not asserted as a fact. The following sentences confirm this observation:

78. *ez dut uste harena den.*

    I do not believe that it is his.

79. *uste dut harena dela.*

I believe that it is his.

We can generalize that *la* serves as a complementizer when the embedded
sentence is asserted as fact and *en* serves as a complementizer when it
is not asserted as a fact. As I have pointed out above, the non-
factive nature of the *en*-complement is determined by the semantic content of the head noun of the complement structure. Sentence 78 makes
it clear that *negation* also plays a role in the creation of non-factive
complements, when verbs of positive assertion *dakit* "I know" and *uste
dut* "I believe" are negated.

2.035  The non-factive complementizing suffix *en* is generally
described in traditional Basque grammars as the affix of the conjunctive, of the subordinate conjugation. Enormously long paradigms are
created by suffixing this ending to otherwise harmless verbs. I identified above the complementizing *la* with the allative postposition *-la,
-lat, -ra, -rat* "to, toward." This says that when a factive noun
phrase complement is extraposed, it is inserted under the locative node
and affixed with a locative postposition. This would seem to be an
audacious assertion. This is harder to accept in the case of *en*-com-
plementation. The seeming formal identity of the *en* of the conjunctive forms with the *en* of the relative nominal forms makes the locative
interpretation a little suspect. However, if we assume that the *en* of
the conjunctive form of the verb is identical with the inessive postposition *n*, it all becomes very clear. This would make the historical
assertion that the formal identity of the genitive in *en* and the conjunctive termination *en* are of relatively recent origin. In order to
appreciate the full operation of this sort of operation, let us examine
some extensions of *la* complementation.

80. *ez dut utzi zure ikustera.*

I didn't let him see you.

81. *entxeatu da jatera.*

He tried to eat it.

82. *etorri zen bertze mandozainaren atxemaitera.*

    He went to find the other mule-driver.

83. *zertako jin dira gure bakearen nahastera*

    Why have they come to spoil our peace?

I propose in Figures 45, 46, and 47 the following underlying structure
for sentence 80 which represents the embedding of

84. *harek zu ikusten zitu.*

    He sees you.

in a matrix sentence:

85. *ez dut (nik) hura utzi.*

    I have not let him.

The transformations that lead from the underlying structure in Figure
45 to the final structure in Figure 47 are essentially identical with
those for *la*-complementation. They, so to speak, take the transformation a few steps further. And, too, the structural description of the
structures to be transformed differs strongly from the structures subject to straight *la*-complementation. It must be noted that the agent
of the embedded sentence is identical with the animate object of the
matrix sentence. When this structural description is met, the *la*-
complementation transformation is extended inasmuch as it removes all
proper verbal inflection from the verb complex of the embedded sentence, yielding a nominalized verb. It must be added at this point
that the verbal affix *te*, which has the variants *ite*, *tze* in other
classes of verbs, plays an important role in other forms of nominaliza-
tion and the development of tense indicators.

   The steps in this transformation are:

a. Extraposition of the noun phrase complement to locative node.

b. Affixation of locative postposition *la*.

c. Obligatory removal of verbal auxiliary in embedded sentence.

d. Genitivization of objective noun in embedded sentence.

   2.036 One of the underlying functions assumed in the Fillmore
hypothesis is that of a noun phrase marked *dative*, defined above as

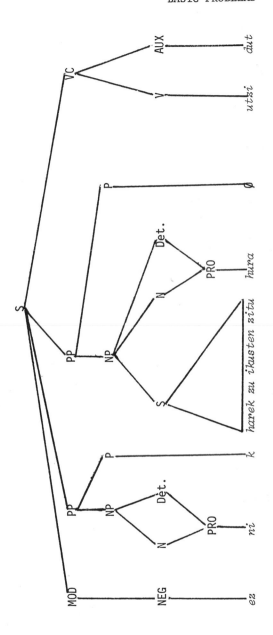

Figure 45

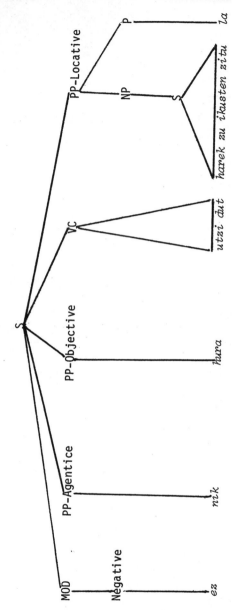

Figure 46

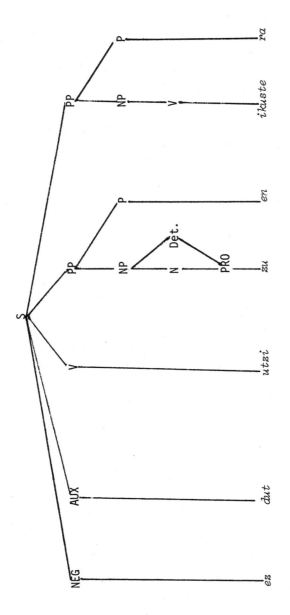

Figure 47

"the case of the animate being affected by the state or action identified by the verb." Just which noun phrase is *dative* is not always immediately evident from the surface structure.[11] It may turn out that
the term for this underlying function really disguises more than one
underlying function or *case*. At this point, I shall assume only a
*dative node* at the beginning of each derivation, looking all the time
for evidence that indeed there are really two or more labels necessary
for this node. Let us examine the following sentences:

86. *lasterrik etzaion bihi bat.*

    Soon he did not have a single one (left).

87. *lasterrik etzuen bihi bat*

    Soon he did not have a single one.

A tree diagram of the surface structure of each of the two sentences
will yield as shown in Figures 48 and 49. Although the surface description of these two sentences would make them seem quite different,
a very likely thesis is that they have the same deep structure. According to this idea, the pronominal forms *harek,* an *ergative,* and
*hari,* a *dative,* are surface realizations of a single underlying relationship. In the first sentence, 86, the verb realized is the *transitive* verb of traditional grammar, while in the second sentence, 87,
the verb realized is the *intransitive* verb of traditional grammar.
However, the real relationship in the sentence is the relationship
between the *person* and the *thing*. The verb realized is only a tense
carrier and a vehicle for showing pronoun reflexes of the surface
realizations of noun phrases. It is an *empty verb*. And it is chame-
leon-like in its behavior, for, in itself, it is devoid of content.
For the underlying structure of both sentences 86 and 87, we can posit
the structures as in Figure 50. This will necessitate a slight modification of the definition of the *underlying case dative*, for there is,
according to the hypothesis presented, no verb present. What is expressed by sentences of the structure posited is the relationship between two noun phrases. This infers that all animate genitive constructions contain embedded sentences of this structure.

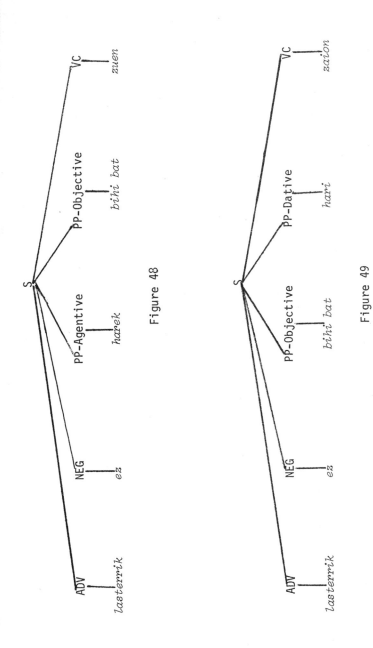

Figure 48

Figure 49

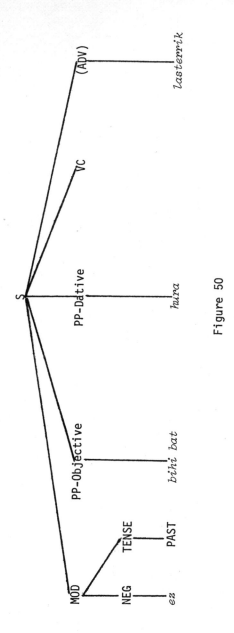

Figure 50

2.037    The immediate problem is to pose an hypothesis to account
for the occurrence sometimes of a surface *ergative* and sometimes of a
surface *dative* in independent realizations of such sentences.  One way
of account for this phenomenon is to assume that a feature is added to
the dative noun phrase.  This feature can be called *focus*.  I shall
posit the notion that focus is not a semantic feature of the sentence
itself, but a feature of the discourse in which the sentence appears.
This is a feature that is added by the context of communication.  It
resembles in its manner of operation features of prosody, emphasis,
hesitation, irony, and endearment.  It is added, so to speak, from
above.  As far as the sentence is concerned, it amounts to an optional
stylistic device with immediate syntactic results.  Inasmuch as the
*hari*, a surface dative, is the syntactic realization of an underlying
dative, we can say that sentence 86 is the "normal" realization of the
underlying structure in Figure 50, while sentence 87 represents the
"abnormal" realization of the underlying structure.  In other words,
sentence 87 is semantically more marked.  The fact that an alternate
surface realization is possible makes it necessary for us to insist
upon the operation, *focus determination*.  The problem to be settled
is whether every sentence has a focus or whether only some sentences
are thus marked.  For the moment I shall assume that every sentence is
somehow focused.  After the focus determination has been made in sentence 86 we must assume that the focus is upon the inanimate noun
phrase labeled objective in deep structure.  In this case, *hura* is
realized on the surface as dative, *hari*, in an operation we can designate as "normal" or "unmarked."  Since no agentive surface marker, no
ergative, is present in the surface realization of the sentence, *kio*
is realized in the so-called intransitive auxiliary *izan* in this particular tense and mood.  This yields a string *izan* + *kio* + 3PERS + OBJ
+ PAST; this is realized phonologically as *zaion*.  If, on the other
hand, the animate person is chosen as focus, *hura* is assigned to the
ergative case on the surface, which is realized as *harek*.  At the same
time, an indicator of the ergative third person singular is inserted

in the verbal auxiliary. In traditional terms the auxiliary is then
a member of the paradigm of the transitive auxiliary *izan*. The auxiliary then consists of a string:  *izan* + 3PERS ERG + 3PERS OBJ + PAST,
which is realized as *zuen*.

2.038  This sort of behavior is not at all confined to sentences
with empty verbs. Note the following sentences containg the verbs
*argitu* "to shine," *laket* "to be pleased," *higuin* "to be displeased, to
dislike." I shall designate the auxiliary as transitive in parentheses.

88. *bekhatuan laketzen zaio.*  (intransitive)

It pleases him (to remain) in sin.

89. *laket dut heiekin.*  (transitive)

I like it (to stay) with them.

90. *higuintzen zaizkit plazerak.*  (intransitive)

The pleasures disgust me.

91. *haren egiteak higuintzen ditut.*  (transitive)

I dislike his goings on.

92. *iguzkiak argitzen du eta zerua argitzen da.* (transitive and in-
                                                  transitive)

The sun is shining away and the sky is sparkling.

It would seem that in these pairs of sentences, the members with noun
phrases marked with the ergative case have a more intense meaning.
The following sentences are particularly revealing of this particular
grammatical process:

93a. *nor zira?*

Who are you?

93b. *nor zaitugu?*

Who are you? (Literally: Who do we have you?)

94a. *haurrak Baionan nituen.*

94b. *ene haurrak Baionan ziren.*

94c. *haurrak Baionan zaiztan.*

My children were in Bayonne.

2.039  The sentences 93a and 93 b bring us to a special class of
sentences.  In addition to being interrogative, it is a sentence that
makes an identification of individuality and class.  Perhaps a better
example would be the following two sentences:

95a. *haren semea apheza da.*

95b. *semea apeza du.*

His son is a priest.

Such sentences belong to the class of pure predications: *"X belongs
to the class Y."*  This sort of sentence is difficult to treat in terms
of case grammar.  It must be added that pure predications make up the
subject material of Aristotle's Categories and, consequently, of classical syllogistic logic.  Although such sentences are awkward to
handle in terms of case grammar, one possibility is the positing of
an *essive* case.  It seems possible to set up this case that can occur
only under very strict circumstances.  These can be illustrated by
setting up a diagram of the underlying structure of sentences 95a and
95b in Figure 51.  Of course this diagram contradicts one of the basic
tenets of case theory, namely, that an underlying case occurs only
once in the deep structure of a simplex sentence.  If we posit an
essive case, then it must occur when and only when two identical underlying cases must be posited.  Then the label of the right-handed node
is changed to *essive* as in Figure 52.  The essive case will dominate
what is called the *predicate nominative* in traditional grammar.  However, this statement concerns only *nominal predicate nominatives*.  Adjectival predicate nominatives are of quite a different sort.  The
relationship between subject and predicate or, in our terms, dative/
objective and essive brings us to the structure of the lexicon and
ultimately to the structure of reality.  These are subjects far beyond
the modest scope of this study.  The essive of sentences 93a and 93b
resembles in its behavior the locative of sentence 94b, as shown in
Figures 53 through 56.  Sentence 94c represents an interesting variant
inasmuch as the adnominal dative is raised to a sentence dative, yielding the structure in Figure 56.

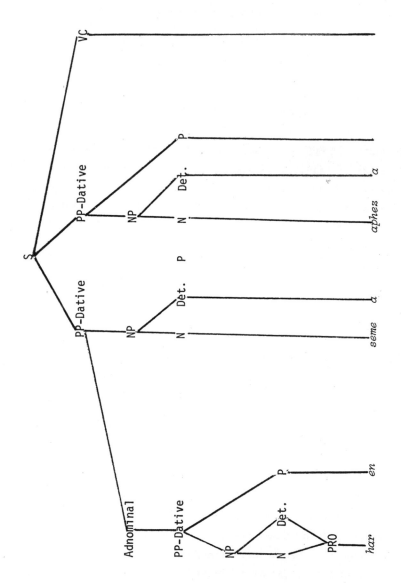

Figure 51

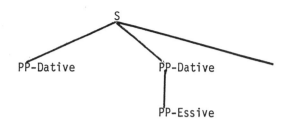

Figure 52

2.040   There are certain verbs that are restricted in this respect.   In a very strict sense, they are exceptional verbs.   For instance, the verbs *maite* "to like, to love" and *plazer* "to be pleased"
realize an underlying dative exclusively as a surface ergative.   Note
the following sentences:

96. *nik zakurra maite dut.*

   I like the dog1

97. *plazer dut zure ezagutzea.*

   I am pleased (to make) your acquaintance.

Forms such as the following never occur:

98. *\*zakurra eni maite zait.*

99. *\*zure ezagutzea eni plazer zait.*

These are but two representatives of a group of exceptional verbs
called *deponents* by Lafitte (1963:189-190).   He lists them as follows:
*afaldu* "to eat dinner"; *argitu* "to shine, to sparkle"; *askaldu* "to eat
breakfast"; *beilatu* "to sit up"; *berandu* "to grow late"; *buhatu* "to
blow"; *dirdiratu* "to shine, to glow"; *distiratu* "to flash, to spark";
*dudatu* "to doubt"; *eman* "to blow (of the wind)"; *erreusitu* "to succeed";
*hartu* "to take root"; *gosaldu* "to eat breakfast"; *iduritu* "to resemble";
*ihardoki* "to resist"; *irakitu* "to boil"; *iraun* "to last"; *izarniatu* "to

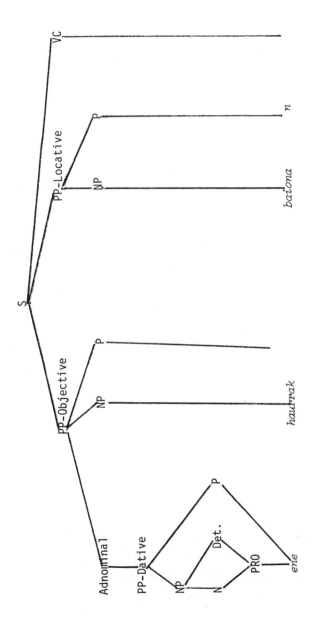

Figure 53

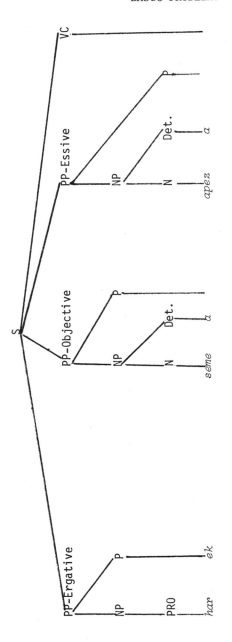

Figure 54

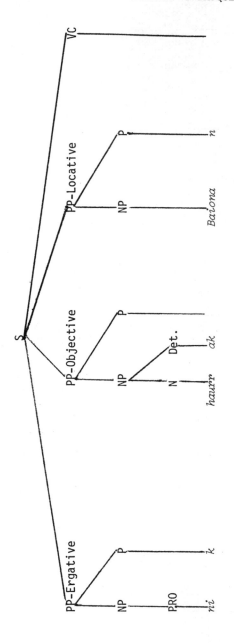

Figure 55

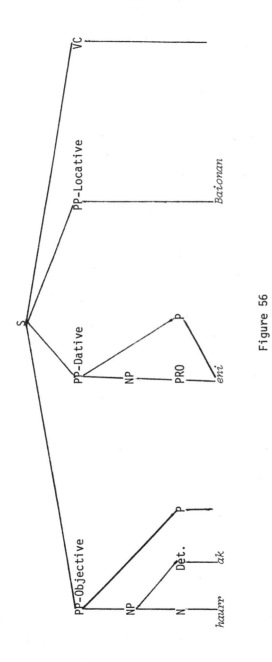

Figure 56

sparkle, to shimmer"; *jazarri* "to resist"; *kurritu* "to run"; *laboratu* "to labor, to drudge"; *laketu* "to be pleased"; *luzatu* "to drag out"; *pausatu* "to alight"; *berdatu, perdatu* "to become green"; *usatu* "to do something habitually".

2.041  It is really exceptional when a verb determines the occurrence of the surface cases of its associated noun phrases. As I have tried to show above the situation is usually determined by other factors, for most Basque verbs are free of such constraining behavior. I wish to exclude from this statement the many cases that are illustrated by the verb *beha*:

100. *beha niri!*

Look at me!

101. *zure beha nindagon.*

I was waiting for you.

In these particular cases, there is a kind of semantic split between *beha* + dative "to look at" and *beha* + genitive "wait for." I shall treat such verbs as *complex verbs* similar in structure to verbs in English such as *look at, look up, wait for, wait on,* where each complex verb has a different semantic content. By such a treatment, we again establish the functional identity of the postposition and preposition. While it is convenient to refer to the verb in sentence 100 as *beha* + dative, it is more accurate to refer to it as *beha* + *-i*.

2.042  The exceptional verbs are those that require the appearance of surface case forms that somehow contradict the logical reality that most case forms, underlying and surface, betray. The semantic content of the sentence structure--in contrast to the *meaning* of the entire sentence--is that set of relationships that subsists between the verb and each of the noun phrases associated with it and, in addition, those relationships among the noun phrases themselves. In this sense, the sentence is a self-contained whole. In terms of pragmatics and discourse structure, it certainly is not. While it is true that certain verbs because of their semantic content will rarely occur with a noun phrase marked for agentive, this possibility is not blocked

a priori in Basque.  The so-called transitive uses of the verbs *joan*
"to go" and *heldu* "to come" are very revealing of this possibility.
102. *joan da.*

    He has gone.
103. *joan du.*

    He took it away.
104. *heltzen da.*

    He is coming.
105. *heltzen daut.*

    He is sending it to me.
It is most important to observe that the true sense of the "animate
instigator" contained in the agentive case is most vividly revealed
by these pairs of sentences.  It is totally unnecessary to impose
upon the grammatical description of the verb some sort of secondary
causative sense or to posit a supraordinate causative sentence such as
106. [he causes it [it comes / goes]$^S$]$^S$
As a matter of fact, this would ultimately force us to presuppose such
a supraordinate sentence for every single sentence that contains a
noun phrase marked for agentive.  The strictures of the grammarian's
metaphysical definitions will in no wise impede the creative processes
of language when it is operating with its own means.

    2.043  This was the purpose of my early introduction into this
discussion of the dispute about the importance of *status* in the classification of Basque verbs.  Basque verbs are neither transitive nor
intransitive.  Insistence upon classifying all verbs under one of these
two rubrics will lead to such self-contradictory statements as: "This
is an intransitive verb used transitively."  In support of this line
of argument, I shall return to sentences 7, *gizona oihanean galdu da,*
and 8, *gizonak oihanean galdu du,* and their analyses in Figures 5 and
6.  Let us replace these latter analyses with case-grammar analyses,
as shown in Figures 57 and 58.  It seems that it is the presence or
absence of the grammatical ergative case that determines the form of
the inflected verb.  The traditional classification of auxiliaries

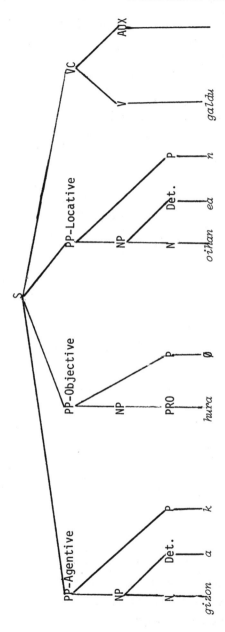

Figure 57

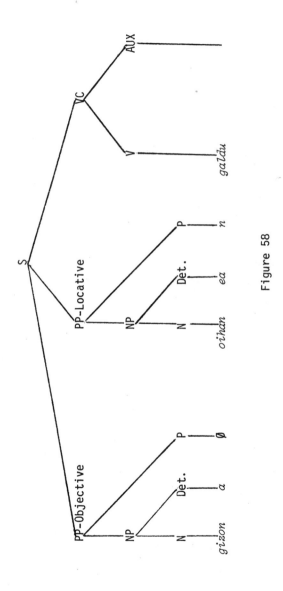

Figure 58

and root-inflecting verbs into two sorts, transitive and intransitive,
is based solely upon this criterion. Since there are at least two
other parameters of verbal inflexion, besides indications of tense,
mood, aspect, and negation, those of the dative and allocutive, we
could set up quite justifiable paradigms arranged according to the
presence or absence of indications of the dative. That would simply
represent another principle of ordering with an equal amount of ration-
ality about it. As I have pointed out in a short introductory sketch
of the parameters of verbal inflexion (§2.011), inflected verbs contain pronominal reflexes of the grammatical surface cases, ergative,
neutral, dative, and allocutive. Inflected forms without indication
of allocution will be referred to as *common* or *narrative forms*. These
parameters of verbal inflection certainly present an unfamiliar pattern to speakers of what Benjamin Lee Whorf called Standard Average
European. When the inflected forms of the verb are arranged paradigmatically, the lists become very long and very intricate. In addition,
there are numerous variant forms that give the list the appearance of
extreme paradigmatic instability or irregularity. It is quite apparent that a paradigmatic arrangement, a systematic display of all the
possible forms, dismisses some rather powerful intuitions, for it
fails to provide a definition of the mechanism whereby the forms were
created. I present the thesis that these seemingly complex forms are
created anew for each sentence. Paradigmatic presentation attributes
to the speaker an incredible memory and an even more incredible uncertainty about individual forms. A look-up list of possible forms is
indeed a very handy philological tool. It is not a grammatical tool,
for it tells us nothing about the grammatical processes that the
speaker uses and that the learner must master. According to my thesis,
pronoun reflexes are inserted into the proper verbal form in a given
order after the assignment of surface cases and that, after this insertion certain phonological rules go into operation in a given order
that generates the phonetic shape of the surface form. Some surface
verbal forms are quite easy to analyze while others are not so obvious.

Variant forms must be accounted for by means of the description of
the collision of different rules of ordering in formative and phonetic
elements. These collisions make it very clear that some rather complicated but orderly phonological processes are at work. Another
effect of the collision of rules is the repeated generation of ambiguous forms. For instance, the sentence below can mean "They said it to
him," "He said it to them," and even "They said it to them":
107. *erran zioten.*
In ordinary discourse the form will be immediately disambiguated by
the presence of one or more surface noun phrases. We might also find
for the surface form of the auxiliary the phonetic shapes *zaioten* or
*zakoten.* The more likely form for the third possible interpretation
would be *zioteen.* There is something more going on here than mere
dialect variation. None of the three forms above represents a deflec-
tion from the norm. An exhaustive listing of all possible Basque verb
forms would disclose a great number of such ambiguous realizations.

   2.044 The immediate sources of the pronoun reflexes of the inflected verbal forms, ergative, dative, neutral, in the Basque sentence are readily visible. In terms of transformational grammar, these
reflexes are introduced into the verb complex by a late concord transformation *after the assignment of surface case forms.* The process can
be present in the following scheme, from which, for purposes of illustrative brevity, I have omitted elements of plural indication and
verbal modality, tense, and aspect. The scheme in Figure 59 is both
incomplete and subject to further conflation. The third formula represents a variation that occurs under very strict circumstances:
when one or both of the pronoun reflexes of noun phrases that are
marked on the surface for neutral or ergative case are in the third
person and when the tense is not present indicative.

   2.045 The surface source of the allocutive reflexes is not so
immediately identifiable. It remains hidden. Two potential explanations suggest themselves. We can suppose that the entire sentence is
dominated by a supraordinate sentence with the content "I say to you"

a. Simplex verbs:

###(PP-ERG)##(PP-DAT)##PP-NEUT##V###

###(PP-ERG)##(PP-DAT)##PP-NEUT##PRO-NEUT#V#(PRO-DAT)#(PRO-ERG)###

b. Complex verbs:

###(PP-ERG)##(PP-DAT)##PP-NEUT##V##AUX###

###(PP-ERG)##(PP-DAT)##PP-NEUT##V##PRO-NEUT@AUX#(PRO-DAT)#(PRO-ERG)###

c. Reverse verbs:

##PRO-NEUT# $\left\{\begin{matrix}V\\AUX\end{matrix}\right\}$ #(PRO-DAT)#PRO-ERG##

##PRO-ERG#PRO-NEUT# $\left\{\begin{matrix}V\\AUX\end{matrix}\right\}$ #(PRO-DAT)##

Figure 59

Definitions:

\# = morpheme boundary

\## = word boundary

\### = sentence boundary

or that a *vocative*, a noun phrase with a special case marking, was present in the surface structure of the sentence and was automatically deleted.  Let us explore the two possibilities by examining the following sentence that contains the allocutive verbal form *jakin diat* "I found it out (as far as you, a male, are concerned)."  The auxiliary thus includes pronominal reflexes of ergative, neutral, and allocutive.

108. *holako zubi azpian jakin diat, nola hatxemanen nintuen ene mandoak.*

Under such and such a bridge I found out how I was to get my mules.

According to the first supposition, we might set up the following underlying structure for the sentence in Figure 60.  A derivation starting with this proposed deep structure analysis would require in the early steps the following operations:

a. Lowering of the dative *hiri* into the target sentence.

b. Deletion of the higher sentence $\bar{S}$.

This process would leave us with an intermediate structure of the shape in Figure 61.  The alternate proposal assumes in the underlying structure not a supraordinate sentence, by an asyntactic or parenthetical pronoun, *hi, zu, zuek*.  Sentence 108 would at an earlier stage read something like *\*hi, holako zubi azpian jakin dut* ....  In the course of derivation, *hi* by a concord operation is reflected in the auxiliary, appearing only optionally on the surface.  The difficulty in both assumptions lies in the matter of sex-concord, for the auxiliary *diat* would not occur if the sentence were to be addressed to a woman.  The form would then be *dinat*.  This is the sole case in Basque grammar where anything remotely resembling gender distinction occurs.  Undoubtedly the real solution is historical.  In the independent second person pronoun a masculine-feminine distinction has disappeared.  Perhaps this came about by a process of phonetic merger.  It would be hard to imagine a very late invasion of sex distinction into the pronoun system of an otherwise totally genderless grammar.  Since we have

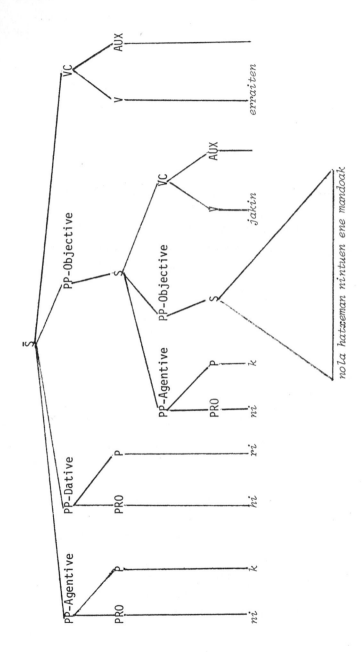

Figure 60

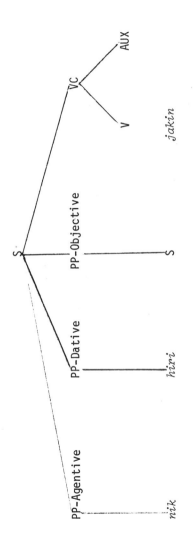

Figure 61

no means of retrieving a very early state of affairs, this must remain a matter of speculation. From a purely synchronic perspective,
we must assume the presence of an opposite NP something like *hi,
gizon!  hi, Martin!* or *hi, emazte!  hi, Emilia!* somewhere in the
derivation. Perhaps the assumption of the presence of a proper name
of an animate being would be the safest assumption inasmuch as such
names are by custom inherently male or female.

  2.046 Another source of dative NP's and their pronominal reflexes is to be found in a special class of sentences, causative sentences. The interrelatedness of *dative* and *ergative* in the surface
realizations of simplex sentences was detailed above in §2.036. What
is important to our observations is the systematic alternation of
ergative and dative in complex sentences of the causative type. The
grammar of Basque contains two immediately apparent kinds of causative
sentences. They are immediately apparent because of the almost transparent morphology of the verb complex in such sentences. These kinds
can be characterized as the prefixing (or compound) causative, e.g.
*ikhasi* "to learn": *erakatsi* "to teach" and the suffixing (or analytic)
causative:  e.g. *jan* "to eat": *jan-arazi* "to feed." This very superficial manner of classification is based simply upon the concatenation
of morphological elements in the verb complex. Sentences that contain
such causative verbs are derived by prefixing and suffixing from other
verbs. They add to our knowledge of the factors that control case-
assignment. An important contribution to the understanding of causative sentences is to be found in Judith Aissen's article (1974:325):
"In various languages of the world, a causative construction is found
which behaves on the surface like a simplex S." This simple and very
deceptive fact led the grammarians of Basque--and those of many other
languages--to treat causative formations as simple cases of word-deriv-
ation to be dealt with in dictionary entries and as sub-entries in
chapters of morphology. It could not occur to them to treat causative
formations as elements in a class of sentences with unique properties.
The following sets of sentences in very formal, even archaic, Basque

will serve to illustrate the composition of non-causative sentences
in contrast to purely causative sentences.
109a. *Antoniok ogia jan du.*
      Antonio has eaten the bread.
109b. *Antoniok untsa jan arazi zaikon.*
      Antonio fed him well.
110a. *hilen dira.*
      They will die.
110b. *hil eraziren dituzte.*
      They will kill them.
110c. *ezadila erhaiten*
      Thou shalt not kill.
111a. *gaur entzunen duzue harramantza.*
      Tonight you will hear the noise.
111b. *erantzuten zioten Jainkoaren hitza.*
      He was announcing to them the word of God.
111c. *gorrei entzun eraziten draue.*
      He makes the deaf hear.
112a. *ikhusiko dugu bihar.*
      We shall see it tomorrow.
112b. *lurrean zerbeit erakusten ziola.*
      As he showed him something on the ground.
113a. *muthikoak laster ikhasi zuen giza hortan Patteria.*
      The boy learned the Lord's Prayer quickly in this way.
113b. *madarikatua gauza hoi erakatsi daukana.*
      Accursed be the one who taught you this thing.
In each of these sets the first sentence (a) represents a non-causative
type. Sentences 109b, 110b, 111b represent suffixing causative verb
types that are formed by suffixing *erazi/ arazi* to the simplex verb.
Sentences 111c, 112b, 113b represent prefixing causative verb types
formed by prefixing *era-/ ira-* to the simple verb. In the case of
110b, 110c, and 111b, 111c, we find that suffixing, prefixing, and lexical causatives can stand side by side, *hil-erazi: erhaiten    entzun-*

*erazi: erantzun.* There is more than a small amount of uncertainty in
Basque orthographic practice about the representation of the suffixing
causative verbs. Most Basque grammarians and lexicographers hedge on
this point by hyphenating the forms as I have, e.g. *egin* "to do": *egin-
arazi* "to cause to do." Modern authors tend to prefer writing the
causative form solid as *eginerazi.* This preference is evidenced in a
recent translation of Franz Kafka's *Die Verwandlung* into Basque (1970:
*Itxura-aldaketa,* 51):

114. ... *baina arin atzeratu behar izan zuen, igurtziak hotzikarak*
     sentierazten *baitzizkion.*

     But he had to draw it [his leg] back immediately, for the contact
     made him feel cold shivers.

This practice tends to disguise the fact that what we find here is not
at all a suffix in the ordinary sense. We find here, rather, a simple
dependent verb construction. The first element is in traditional terms
a dependent infinitive. This is confirmed by de Azkue's remark (1969:
*arazi,* s.v.): "Généralement il se joint à un autre verbe, cependant je
l'ai entendu isolé en Bas Navarrais." He gives the following example:

115. *arazi sugu*

     Nous l'avons obligé.

Lhande (1926: *arazi,* s.v.) includes in his entry a diminutive form of
the causative verb without a dependent infinitive:

116. *lanian arazixetan titzu.*

     Il est arrivé à les faire travailler un peu.

These two spare examples serve to establish *arazi* as an independent
verb. It cannot be considered as a simple derivative suffic. Prefixing causatives, on the other hand, belong properly within the sphere of
derivational morphology. By regular processes of derivation *ikhusi,*
the infinitive-participial form of the verb "to see" (the dictionary
form of a Basque verb) and its causative partner *erakutzi* "to cause to
see, to show" are both derived from a root *kus,* which Basque lexicographers characterize as "idea of seeing" (Lhande, 1926: *ikhus,* s.v.).
However, this particular kind of derivation is no longer productive.

Lafitte (1963:38) remarks:

> Beaucoup de verbes factitifs de forme ne le sont pas de sens.
> ... iragon, factitif de egon, *rester*, ne signifie pas *faire res-*
> *ter*, mais *durer*. Noter, d'autre part, qu'aujourd'hui on fait
> les nouveaux factitifs à l'aide du suffixe -erazi signale plus
> haut. De higitu, *remuer*, on tirerera higi-arazi, *faire remuer*;
> une forme comme erhigitu ne serait comprise par personne.

Nevertheless, any number of the prefixing forms do remain immediately
comprehensible in a purely causative sense, e.g. *ahatzi* "to forget":
*erahatzi* "to cause to forget." Almost spitefully, the transparent
sense of the causative can stand right beside idiosyncratic expansions
of meaning. For example in the pair, *ebaki* "to cut": *erabaki* "to cause
to cut" we find sentences with a clearly causative interpretation and
sentences with a highly "idiomatic" derived sense:

117. *burua erabaki zion.*

   He made him cut his head.

118. *erabaki zuten etsaia igurikitzera.*

   They decided to wait for the enemy.

As a noun *erabaki* is glossed as "judgment, decision" (Lhande, 1926,
s.v.). For these reasons we must conclude that prefixing causatives
properly belong the lexicon as separate entries. In short, we are
dealing with an historical phenomenon. What was once a productive
process of derivation, has been removed to the lexicon. As Lafitte
points out above the speaker of Basque can no longer freely create prefixing causative forms of the verb. This fact is particularly irritat-
ing because the process is still fully transparent. A superficial inspection of the processes of Basque morphology will reveal that prefixing seems to play a role, but a very small one, in an otherwise extremely productive system. The one striking exception to this observation
is to be found in the ordering of connectives and clitic pronominal
elements in the verbal auxiliary. In other classes of words, the use
of prefixation is downright suspicious. Where prefixation does occur,
it seems to be in the greater number of cases an out-and-out borrowing

from Romance, e.g. Rom. *re-*, *ré-*, *ra:* Basque *erre-*, *arra-* as found in
*maiatz* "May": *arramaitz* "June"; *berri* "new": *erreberritu* "renew."
The same formation occurs with the native *ber-*, *bir-* "two, twice,"
e.g. *hogoi* "twenty": *berhogoi* "forty"; *landatu* "to plant": *birlandatu*
"transplant." Such formations undoubtedly represent loan translations.
Another borrowing from Romance is to be found in *des-*, e.g. *egin* "to
do": *desegin* "to undo"; *herri* "country": *desherri* "exile." The same
formation is to be found making use of the native *ez-* "no, not," e.g.
*jakin* "to know, known": *ezjakin* "unknowing, ignorant"; *ontsa* "well":
*ezontsa* "sickness." These formations are relatively late and superficial borrowings from the neighboring Romance dialects. One apparently very productive native prefix is *bas(a)* "wild," e.g. *ahate* "duck":
*basahate* "wild duck"; *ahalge* "shame": *basahalge* "false shame." If Lafitte (1963:38) in his surmise that *bas(a)* is a compounding form of
*baso* "forest," it must follow that this is not a case of prefixing at
all, but a case of normal nominal compounding. It is, however, possible to discover a much older layer of derivational processes in the
formation of verbal nouns, i.e. infinitives. From the roots *kus* "to
see, *ros* "to buy," *ma* "to give" are derived the infinitival forms
*ikusi*, *erosi*, *eman*, where *i*, *e* is prefixed to the root and *i* is suffixed to roots that terminate in a consonant while *n* is suffixed to
roots that terminate in a vowel. (The terminal *i* is omitted in case
of the so-called radical infinitive.) The same prefixed *e*, *i* is observed in any number of nouns, e.g. *ibai* "river"; *igel* "frog (*gel*,
*igeri* "to swim"); *euri* "rain." Since this kind of derivation is no
longer productive, it has been replaced by a more recent and fully productive nominalizing formation, whereby *tu(du)* is suffixed to the
verbal root whatever its historical origin, e.g. *euritu* "to rain." In
the course of time, Basque has eliminated prefixing as a manner of
derivation. The remainders of the older state of affairs have been
completely lexicalized. From an historical point of view, it is interesting that a former system can be partially retrieved. This interesting fact permits us to reconstruct--in rather vague outlines--

the process of a typological switch.  Judith Aissen (1973:325) analyzes
the superficially simplex causative sentences (her examples are drawn
primarily from Turkish and French) as having a bisentential underlying
structure of the following form:

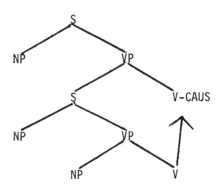

Figure 62

The lower, embedded S is raised into the matrix S, yielding a derived
structure of the following form which Aissen (1973:331) describes as a
phrase structure analysis of verb-raising causatives:

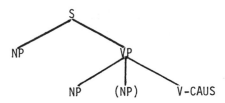

Figure 63

A casual inspection of the Basque sentences above will show that such a linear analysis seems to fit rather neatly the facts of Basque causative sentences.  In order to derive sentence 112b, for instance, we could assume that in a matrix sentence that might be realized as:

119. *harek[1] erazi zuen.*

    He caused it.

is embedded the sentence that might be realized as:

120. *harek[2] lurrean zerbeit ikhusi zuen*

    He saw something on the ground.

When the verb is raised *(i)kus(i)* + CAUSE yields the compound verb *erakutsi*.  When the NP, *harek[2]*, is raised, it is assigned the dative case.  This yields a bracketed string:  [NP[1] - ERG [NP[2] - DAT + NP - INESSIVE + NP - Ø + V] CAUSE].  This same derived structure could in Modern Basque produce the perfectly acceptable sentence:

121. *harek lurrean zerbeit ikusi erazi zaikon.*

    He made him see something on the ground.

The bisentential analysis simply points up two simple facts:

a. Surface causal structures are embedding structures of the general
   form:  $^S$[NP $^{VP}$[ $^S$[NP $^{VP}$[(NP) V]$^{VP}$]$^S$ CAUSE]$^{VP}$]$^S$.

b. The proposed V(erb)-R(aising) rule changes the constituent verb
   and the matrix verb into a unit of some sort.

It is Aissen's argument (1973:339) that VR is a universal rule while the arrangement of morphological elements in the realized sentence is language-particular.  However, I think it is necessary to cast doubt upon the bisentential analysis.  I anticipated this doubt in §2.042. It is precisely the examples in that section, sentences 102 to 105, that permit this.  Note in particular:

    102. *joan da.*

        He has gone.

    103. *joan du.*

        He took it away.

The latter sentence could be interpreted as "He caused it to go (away)." It is precisely here that we see that it is unnecessary to assume two sentences that have somehow been pasted together and conflated.  In the

case of sentence 103, we should have to posit a lowered supraordinate
sentence while in the case of 110b and 112b we should have to posit
raised subordinate sentences.  At this point sentential decomposition
becomes suspect.  It is clear enough that the verb forms occurring in
causative sentences have various morphological, i.e. historical,
sources.  To claim that all causative sentences are bisentential leads
to the necessary conclusion that lexical causatives such as *erhain* in
sentence 110c must be decomposed into "cause to die."  This is not an
argument for synchronic above diachronic grammar.  In fact, it is an
historical argument in that it argues that such verbs did not originate
in a bisentential structure.  This argument says also that causative
verbs appear in complex sentences that are complex because the underlying semantic structure is complex.  This is a strong claim that the
human being frames complicated meanings and produces them as one unit.
Underlying a complex sentence is a complex proposition.  In terms of
strict case grammar the verbs can be described as occurring with "complex" verb frames inasmuch as, if the causative verb has a non-causative
partner, the number of nominal arguments in the case-frame is increased
by at least one.  In the causative member of the pair, that extra noun
phrase will indicate the agent that brings about the action, the causer.
In case grammar that noun phrase will be labeled agentive in the underlying structure.  In Basque sentences it will be realized as a noun
phrase with an ergative postposition.  That the abstract element CAUSE
need not be morphologically realized as part of the complex verb is most
strikingly shown by sentence 103.  There are other verbs like this.
Contrast the following sentence with sentences 110a, 110b, 110c:
122. *hil du*.
     He killed it.
Sentence 103 could be expanded as "He caused or instigated the event
that it was gone," and sentence 122 could be expanded as "He caused or
instigated the event that it died."  The situation becomes more interesting when the event is represented by a non-causative verb requiring
the presence of an ergative (agentive) in its frame, i.e. a transitive

verb.  Note the pair of sentences, 109a and 109b.  The non-causative *jan* is accompanied by the ergative *Antoniok*.  When the causative *janarazi* is accompanied by *Antoniok* it indicates that Antonio caused another person to eat.  If that other person caused Antonio to eat, the sentence would read as follows:

123. *(Harek) Antoniori jan arazi zaikon.*

In the realized sentence, the second agent is realized as a dative. This follows from the proviso in case grammar that one case may only occur once in a particular verb frame.  The interaction and at times interchangeability of agentive and dative found discussion above in

It is simply not necessary to hold that an underlying ergative has been raised or lowered to a dative.  The presence of two animate agents in a complex proposition has been disambiguated by the use of both animate cases.  Since the ergative position is filled, the other animate case is employed.  This pattern represents a kind of template for causative constructions.  This observation leads to the conclusion that there is a typology of sentential types, behind each of which lies a type of logical proposition.  This idea has been developed from the point of view of modern logic in the work of Renate Bartsch and Theo Vennemann (1972), Theo Vennemann (1973), and from a broad comparative point of view in the work of Bernard Comrie (1974, 1976).

# III. SUMMARY AND CONCLUSIONS

3.000   In the course of this essay I have set out to interpret a
number of facts about the grammatical behavior of noun phrases in
Basque.  At no point has the attempt been made to be or even to appear
to be exhaustive.  Instead, on the basis of a finite body of evidence,
I have tried to define a number of linguistically significant generalizations about the constitution of sentences that will stand as a frag-
ment of Basque grammar.  The initial framework chosen for the presentation of the materials was case grammar as expounded by Charles Fillmore.
This choice was determined by the simple fact that many features of
Basque grammar seemed so easy to handle by means of this approach to
grammar.  Indirectly, application of the terms of case grammar to the
materials of Basque will, of course, imply a critique of that framework.
As linguists we are caught between the twin aims of presenting the
materials of a particular language in an efficient manner and of adher-
ing to a consistent theoretical point of view, or at least, of develop-
ing a consistent theory while we are underway.  Perhaps the terms of
case grammar are weak enough to stimulate a great deal of insightful
work in the field of linguistics, which today is a battleground of a
host of contending formal theories.  And it is good scientific practice
to accept a theory provisionally and to see just how far it will take
us.  Recently, Fillmore has closely restricted the claims of case
grammar:

> It was misleading for me to use the phrase CASE GRAMMAR to
> describe the proposals I made in "The Case for Case."  My
> proposals did not cohere into a model of grammar.  Instead
> they were suggestions about a level of organization of a

> clause that was relevant to both its meaning and its grammati-
> cal structure; that provided a way of describing certain
> aspects of lexical structure; and that offered convenient
> classification of clause types. . . . I have become aware
> that my writings somehow have the impression that case gram-
> mar so-called was being presented as a general model of
> linguistic structure. (1977:62)

The fact that case grammar, which we may now safely call the Case Hypothesis, does not cohere into a complete model might be considered to be
its major attraction. The intuitive attraction it has exerted upon
many scholars is clear to see. It is that intuition that led to the
battle in the orthodox transformationalist camp between the Generative
Semanticists and the Interpretivists, and to many other deviations of
greater or lesser degree from the Strict Generativist-Transformational-
ist school. It would seem that in more recent times, every linguist
worth his salt is setting out to found his own formal theory of grammar,
which is a sign that the science is in strapping good health. The intuition in its simplest form is that the input to any syntactic process
is meaning, or in more formal terms all syntactic processes operate on
a semantic base. (Just what that semantic base might be and how it is
to be formulated is the real center of debate.)    A very sophisticated
statement of the basic intuition was best expressed by Bartsch and
Vennemann (1972:8-9):

> The psychological interpretation of sentence generation in
> [Chomsky's] model is that a speaker, when he is about to
> express a certain meaning in his native language, has the
> task of generating a deep structure that has this meaning
> as its semantic representation. How can he do this?
> Since semantic rules are purely interpretive, he must
> randomly generate deep syntactic structures until he acci-
> dentally hits upon one which is assigned the intended mean-
> ing by the semantic rules.

In drastically simple terms, the point of view taken here holds that the syntactic component directly joins two very concrete things, meaning and sound. Meaning is the input for production and sound, or the graphic representation, is the input for understanding. This point of view has one advantage that must be emphasized. If we accept meanings as concrete and as end-products of psychic processes outside the realm of linguistic investigation, we keep ourselves safe from the dangers of gratuitous psychologizing. We shall not fall into the bottomless pit of holding that "linguistics . . . is simply the subfield of psychology that deals with these aspects of the mind" (Chomsky 1968:24). If linguistics confuses itself with psychology, then it denies those data to that science that will be necessary for it to construct its own appropriate theories. If we consider meaning as concrete and discrete and free of any psychological distortions, then that meaning can be represented, without regard to its truth in reality or who produced it or why, in great structural detail by one means or the other. This then is the real problem of THE appropriate semantic representation. The investigator need only comply with Hjelmslev's three requirements for a linguistic theory: arbitrariness, appropriateness, and simplicity. It follows that two or more forms of representation that comply with equal efficiency to these requirements will be isomorphic. It is this ideal semantic representation that is converted by the syntactic and phonological components into linguistic representation. If we read Fillmore's statements carefully, we note that he is not concerned with the problem to the extent that one might expect. He even chides Cook for reading the hypothesis in that manner:

> Walter Cook . . . claims to be taking a position in opposition
> to mine in a postulate which assigns centrality to semantics,
> not syntax. I suspect that if I knew precisely what it
> meant, Cook's is a position I might take, too. But, in any
> event, it was not an opposition between semantics-at-the-
> bottom and syntax-at-the-bottom that I had in mind, but
> rather between analysis that begins with the morpheme and
> analysis that begins with the sentence. (1977:63)

This sounds like refusing to face questions he brought up in the first place. In fact, "The Case for Case" can be easily read as "The Case for Universal Semantics." However, the former statement above reads like a timid withdrawal from the consequences of the original hypothesis. However, let us sum up the results of what may only turn out to be a description of "certain aspects of lexical structure" and offers "convenient classifications of clause types."

3.001  Throughout this essay the linearization of the constituents of every kind and at every level has been treated in a loosely ordered fashion. This is in accord with my conviction that, if there is any ordering of surface placement rules, that ordering is intrinsic.. It will ease presentation to arrange the steps from the proposed deep structures to the surface structures as if they were extrinsically ordered. The most convenient procedure is to present these steps first in the form of rewrite rules and then in the form of transformational rules.

R1.   $S \rightarrow M + Prop.$

According to this rule we separate the proposition from all elements of tense, negation, mood, and modalities in the strict sense of the word (assertion, interrogation, suggestion, possibility, necessity, permission) treating them as operators on the proposition as a whole. Since the Modal component operates primarily on the verb in Basque, this aspect has been totally passed over in this essay. I have confined the discussion to the categorial component that treats of the relationships between noun phrases and verbs.

R2.   $Prop. \rightarrow C^1 + C^2 + \ldots + C^n$

C represents a case-marked NP or PP, with the provision that no two C's are the same in any one proposition. This would seem to indicate that the number of C's in a proposition is theoretically infinite. However, the theory posits a limited, but undefined number of case-roles for the entire grammar. This theoretical presupposition as well as common sense demands that there be a manageable number. I believe that there is internal evidence to the effect that there is a real limitation to the number of PP's in an atomic proposition, viz., if there are more than

three, those PP's are embeddings of other atomic propositions, that is,
we are dealing with a complex proposition.

R3.   PP → NP + K

In Basque K is represented on the surface by a postposition.  The choice
of the postposition we must assume to be assigned in deep-structure, for
it represents the functional relationship that NP bears to the verb.  In
accord with the Case Hypothesis that case indicator has semantic content, the case role imposed upon the real situation by the human
observer.  The case marked PP will be best represented as follows:

R3'.   NP + A, NP + Obj., NP + Dat.

The next step requires place-assignment rules.  A casual inspection of
any lengthy Basque text might give the impression that the relative
order of NPs and the VC within the Basque sentence is a matter of indif-
ference, while on the other hand the order of elements within the NP is
fixed and the order within the VC is looser, but only within very strict
limits.  Experience plus a good dose of intuition shows us that there
is a "normal" or "unmarked" order of elements.  And this order follows
rather well what the typologists characterize as the SOV language type,[12]
or what will serve for our purposes, a verb-last language.  Rudolf P. G.
de Rijk in an article "Is Basque an S.O.V. Language?" (1969:319-351)
gave all the decisive evidence to support what everybody intuited anyway.
Placement rules must be posited about relative position of the NP to the
verb, reading from right to left.  In perfectly neutral, unmarked sentence in Basque, the order of constituents is:  NP-erg. + NP-dat. -
NP-neut. + VC.  This infers that deviation from this order is determined
by other factors such as focus, emphasis, topicalization.[13]  What must
be determined is what the normal position of NP-loc. will be in this
little scheme.  That must be postponed.

The minimal Basque sentence is NP + V.  Since the relationship is
the first modification of the V, it is marked neutral.  This binding
of the two terms is the nucleus to which all placement rules apply.

R4.   NP-dat. is placed immediately to the left of [NP-neut. + VC],
      if NP-dat. is present in the proposition, yielding

[NP-dat. [NP-neut. + VC]].

R5.  NP-erg. is placed immediately to the left of the others,
     yielding [NP-erg. [NP-dat. [NP-neut. + VC]]].

Such an ordering of the syntactic cases infers that placement of other
C's must be accounted for by insertion rules.  This manner of indicating
the serial occurrence of case-marked noun phrases tells us that only
NP-neut. is directly and independently related to the verb.  The other
NP's are related only indirectly.  This result is best presented in the
fashion adopted by Wallace Chafe (1970:150 *et passim*).

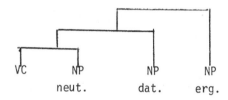

Figure 64

A hierarchy of additions is shown.  Whether such a formulation will
prove to be adequate for more complex representations remains to be in-
vestigated.  Expressed in the modifier-modified terminology, the representation says that NP-neut. modifies VC; that NP-dat. modifies [NP-
neut. + VC]; that N:-erg. modifies [NP-dat. [NP-neut. + VC].  (Extraposition can be defined as any movement of NP's out of this canonical
order.)  In other words, the complement of the head of the construction
moves to the left, step by step, while the composition of the head of
the construction increases in complexity.  It could also be expressed
inversely by saying that NP-erg. has the greatest scope, ergo the
greatest force, of the three syntactic cases.  The limitation that
places only these three cases in the nuclear proposition is quite
natural inasmuch as only these three case-forms are repeated in

pronominal form in the verb complex.

The most troublesome placement rule to define is one to insert the non-syntactic cases, those with semantic content, into the unmarked chain of case-marked noun phrases. These non-syntactic cases are secondary additions to the proposition, being ultimately derived from atomic propositions that act as operators on nuclear propositions. The relationship can be stated in this fashion: [Prop.$^2$ [Prop.$^1$]], where Prop.$^2$ is a complement to Prop.$^1$. The structure of the complementary proposition is NP + K, where K functions as the VC in a nuclear proposition, i.e. as head of construction. Therefore the designation *neutral* is shown to be dispensable, for the structural parallelism is maintained: NP is to VC as NP is to K. The fact that the so-called neutral case is unmarked explains itself. It is only marked by the verb. On the basis of that observation and on the basis of such simple sentences as the following:

124. *Soldadoak gau eta egunez hor zauden.*

The soldiers stayed there day and night.

an insertion rule for non-syntactic cases ($K^x$) can be formulated:

R6. $K^x$ (simple or complex) must be inserted between NP-neut. and VC.

A fitting portraiture of the situation would be:

[NP-erg. [NP-dat. [NP--VC]]]
|
[NP-$K^x$]

This configuration indicates that NP-$K^x$ operates on the whole string and indicates the unmarked position of its lexical realization.

3.002 The ordering of constituents achieved in the previous section permits the expansion of those constituents into further constituents.

R7. NP → (Num.) N + Det. + PL

This accords with what is described in section 2.206 (Figure 21).

R8. Det. [± Def., ± Demon., ± near, ± far]

As discussed in section 2.025, the lexical item chosen to fill this slot
is best described in terms of cross-classified features and then pulled
from a look-up type grammar. Ultimately this answer will prove to be
unsatisfactory, for it leaves out the relationship between quantification and demonstration and their interplay with such forms as *guzi* "all",
*oro* "all", *batzu* "some", *guti* "little", *hainitz* "much", *asko* "enough".

    R9.  PL → ± plural.

This analysis assumes that + plural is realized on the surface as a
discrete morpheme. The general pattern of affixation certainly inclines
us to favor such an answer. However, practical synchronic considerations foresee rather complicated allomorphic statements that will result
from this assumption. Again the use of a look-up list where the
lexicalization is chosen on the basis of $[± PL, K]$ is the provisionally
most efficient manner of rule-giving.

    R10.  VC → {finite verb (primitive verb), compound verb}

This says that the choice of one of a limited number of root-inflecting
verbs leads to the realization of VC as a single form to which all elements of concord and modality are affixed. Otherwise the VC is realized
in a bipartite compound form. A very limited number of verb roots occur
in both primitive and compound form.

    R11.  compound verb → nominalized verb + finite verb

    R12.  finite verb → {Lexical Root, Aux. Root / nominalized
            verb ___} + PRO-refl. + [Modality]

The choice of Aux. Root depends upon the components of the modality,
i.e. tense (present, past, eventual, future), mood (indicative, subjunctive, potential, imperative), aspect (progressive, completive). The
position of *potential* in this scheme is not quite certain. Traditional
grammars confuse the picture inasmuch as they align the forms according
to convenient translations into Romance languages. This is no place to
arrange them in a natural fashion. The rule must be stated somewhat
uncritically in the following fashion:

    R13.  Aux. Root → {izan$^{\alpha}$, edin, ukan, izan$^{\beta}$, egin, iron /
           [Modality]

Note that this is not a lexicalization rule. The non-italicized forms
represent classes of possible lexicalization. The two classes of izan
correspond to the classical intransitive and transitive classifications.
The form *egin* is in itself an independent verb with lexical and compound realization, while *iron* is more restricted. Both verbs as auxiliaries are far more less frequently used now than in earlier texts,
which were much more liberal in the use of these and other auxiliaries.
Lafon (1943:vol. II) describes in great detail the earlier state of
affairs.

     R14.  PRO-ref. → (refl.-erg.) + (refl.-dat.) + refl.-neut. +

           PL

As the discussion in section 2.045 shows, this rewrite in no manner
shows the actual order of these reflexes in the affixed forms of
realized finite verbs, for the reflexes occur in different positions in
varying tenses, moods, and aspects. Plurality is particularly vexing in
this regard owing to the fact that its lexicalized occurrence is often
ambiguous and pleonastic both in reference and in position. In a number
of forms the order of elements is immediately evident. However, phonetic and analogical processes often disguise the order. A complete
morphemic analysis of Basque finite verbal forms with rules to account
for each form is an ambitious project that has yet to be accomplished.

     R15.  nominalized verb form → {nominal infinitive (noun), parti-

                           ciple (adjective), radical

                           infinitive}

The realization of K-inessive on the surface is $-n$, which is traditionally interpreted as an old indefinite inessive case. The progressive
aspect corresponds both to English habitual and progressive aspects.[14]
It is a mistake to identify *ikhusten* with the English present participle, for its derivation morphologically and transformationally is
quite different.

     The participle corresponds more or less to the past participle of
English. It is generated regularly with perfect and past tenses. It
is closely related in behavior to the class of adjectives, which will
be discussed below.

The radical infinitive replaces the participle when the auxiliary is izan$^{\beta}$, edin, or diro, i.e. in a VC that is dominated by a modality that contains the features subjunctive, imperative, or potential. With the deletion of the auxiliary, the form serves as the verb complex in proverbs and sentences that express eternal verities as well as very abrupt imperatives.[15]

The application of the previous rules produces a canonical string:

$$(^{np}[(\text{NUM}) + \text{N} + \text{Det.} + \text{PL} + \text{erg.}]^{np}) + (^{np}[ \ldots + \text{dat.}]^{np}) +$$
$$[ \ldots + \text{neut.}]^{np} + (^{np}[ \ldots + \text{K}^{x}]^{np} + {}^{vc}[(\text{non-finite verb}) +$$
$$\text{R} + (\text{ref.-erg}) + (\text{refl.-dat.}) + \text{refl.-neut.} + (\text{refl.-all.}) +$$
$$\text{Modality}]^{vc}] (]) (])^{16}$$

Representation of this bracketed string by a tree diagram proves to be both unwieldy and unrevealing. All further rules, the rules of lexicalization, recursion, and constituent movement operate upon this string.

3.003 The recursive processes of embedding follow the ordering pattern established for Basque, modifier-modified. This can be most clearly seen in the case of relativization (2.029) where the sentence to be embedded is, as modifier, placed to the left of the noun phrase that is to be modified. Relativization can be formalized in the following way:

R16.    $^{np}[^{np}[^{s}[\text{PP} + \text{X} + \text{VC}]^{s}]^{np} \ \ ^{np}[\text{N} + \text{Det.} + \text{X}]^{np}]^{np} \twoheadrightarrow$
     $^{np}[(\text{PRO}) + \text{X} + \text{VC} + \text{Rel.} + \text{N} + \text{Det.} + \text{X}]^{np}$

From the application of this rule a restrictive relative clause results. No movement of constituents is involved, only deletion of the PP to the left that contains among its constituents N to the right. Under circumstances of extreme ambiguity, the deleted PP may be restored as a PRO-form. If, too, an antecedent to N is quite evident, the relativized noun phrase may be reduced to pronominal status by the following operation:

R16a.   $^{np}[(\text{PRO} + \text{X} + \text{VC} + \text{Rel.} + \text{N} + \text{Det.} + \text{N}]^{np} \twoheadrightarrow$
     $^{np}[(\text{PRO} + \text{X} + \text{VC} + \text{Rel.} + \text{Det.} + \text{N}]^{np}$

These operations may be illustrated with the following sentences (cf. sentences 41, 42, 43):

125. *mutikoak erran daut. mutikoak espartin beltzak baditu.*

The boy said it to me.  The boy has black sandals.

126. *espartin beltzak dituen mutikoak erran daut.*

The boy that has black sandals said it to me.

127. *espartin beltzak dituenak erran daut.*

The one that has black sandals said it to me.

The formation of a non-restrictive clause requires removal of the relativized clause from its modifying prenominal position to a delayed position outside of the proposition.  In configurational terms, the relativized clause is removed from the node NP and attached to S on the
right.  The input of R16b is the output of R15.

R16b.   $^{np}[$(PRO) + X + Rel. + N + Det. + X$]^{np}$ $\rightarrow\rightarrow$

$^{s}[$ ... $^{np}[$N + Det. + X$]^{np}$ $^{np}[$X + VC + Rel. + Det. + X$]^{np}]^{s}$

The strictly modifying role of the clause is nullified, making of that
clause a coordinate structure.

128. *Mutikoak erran daut, espartin beltzak dituenak.*

The boy said it to me, the one that has black sandals.

3.004  Sentence 15 in section 2.028 is capable of another realization.  That realization shows the operation of *adjectivization.*

129. *Mutiko espartin beltzak erran daut.*

(It must be pointed out that the *ak* of *beltzak* is not the neutral plural
definite, but the ergative singular definite of *mutikoak*.)  Other
examples of such formations are to be found in such phrases as:

130. *Jaun apetitu hun hura.*

That gentleman with a good appetite.

131. *Epher xango gorribat.*

A red-footed partridge.

In these cases, a movement operation has moved a postpositional phrase
reduced to a noun phrase by deletion of the determiner and case-marker
into the position between N and Det.   This is the normal adjective
position (2.026-2.028).  The evidence introduced above indicates that
an adjective is an inserted or transported noun phrase.  Therefore, in
accord with the view of many syntacticians, e.g. Lakoff 1970:115-136,

*adjective* is only a surface category derived immediately from relative clauses and finally from verbs of a distinctive class (see p. 71).  In order to account for ordinary attributive constructions such as

132.  *gizona ona da.*

The man is good.

we must assume that *ona* is derived from a VC that contains a V with a special feature on it, perhaps [+ ADJ].  The fact that the adjectival component is fully nominal is assured by the fact that it is affixed with a nominal determiner and indications of plurality.  That the adjective is structurally parallel to the participle is shown by the following sentence, where *ontu*, is the participle of *ont* "ripen".

133.  *sagarrak ontuak dira.*

The apples are ripe(ned).

Therefore, the adjective can be considered a varient result of participle formation.  Semantically, the two differ from one another only in the feature [± Change), i.e. an attained state in contrast to a permanent state of being.  Since the participle and its variant the adjective are nominal forms dominated by NP, we can look at predicate noun constructions again (2.039).

134.  *Anderea serora da.*

The lady is a sister (religious).

135.  *Gizona zuhaitza da.*

The man is a tree, i.e. mean, hard.

These facts make the feature [ADJ] inadequate.  A feature [- verbal] will be more apt.  The feature [± Change] must remain one of the variables.  Note these sentences:

136.  *khexu da.*

He is upset.

137.  *khexua da.*

He is irascible.

Sentence 136 is the result of a change, while sentence 137 indicates a permanent state.  We can refer to the nominal forms occurring in these sentences as *predicate nominals*.  We have simply expanded R11, and R15.

We can rewrite R15 as:

R17. (R15) nominalized verb form → {nominal infinite, nominal
predicate, radical infinitive}

We can show how these forms will be lexicalized:

R17a. NomVF → *khexatzen* /    *(khexu)* [+ Verb, + Verbal, + Progres-
sive]

R17b. NomVF → *khexatu* /          [+ Verb, + Verbal]

R17c. NomVF → *khexu* /            [+ Verb, - Verbal, + Change]

R17d. NomVF → *khexu* + Det. + PL /  [+ Verb, - Verbal, - Change]

There are other features of the verb that make the occurrence of a
radical infinitive unlikely.

The attributive predicate nominal (Pred.Nom.) construction is
derived by this operation:

R18. $^S$[N + Det. + PL + K - VC [+ Verb, - Verbal, - Change] ⇥
$^S$[N + Det. + PL + K - Pred.Nom. + Det. + PL + K - izan - K]

Since there is only one NP here, the case assignment is neutral. If,
however, the feature [+ Change] is present, the copying of Det. + PL + K
onto Pred.Nom. is blocked.

R18a. $^S$[N + Det. + PL + K - VC [+ Verb, - Verbal, + Change] ⇥
$^S$[N + Det. + PL + K - Pred.Nom. - izan + neut.]$^S$

Application of this rule produces the grammatical sentences 132, 133,
134, 135, 136, 137. The curious fact is that lexical nouns can be
assigned to V [+ Verb, - Verbal, - Change], which might be more aptly
written as N [+ Verb, - Verbal, - Change]. This leads to the conclusion
that there are degrees of "nounness" and "verbness." We can assume
three nouns in the underlying structure that sentences 95a and 95b from
section 2.039 share.

95a. *Haren semea apheza da.*

95b. *Semea apheza du.*

His son is a priest.

R18b. $^S$[N *(seme)* + Det. + PL + K' - N *(aita)* + Det. + PL + K'' +
N *(apheza)* [+ Verb, - Verbal, - Change]

Case grammar would incline us to assign Dative to K'', which is accept-

able for the immediate purposes.  In terms of CG, the ergative noun
phrase is mapped onto the surface either as an ergative or as a genitive

$\rightarrowtail$ $^s$[NC (*seme*) + Det. + PL + Gen. - N (*aita*) + Det. + PL + neut. -
   N (*apheza*) + Det. + PL + neut. + izan$^\alpha$ - neut.]

or:

$\rightarrowtail$ $^s$[N (*aita*) + Det. Pl. + Erg. - N (*seme*) + Det. + PL + neut. -
   N (*apheza*) + Det. + PL + neut. + izan$^\beta$ + neut. + erg.]

In sentence 95b the ergative noun phrase is optionally deleted because
it is clearly reflected in the finite verb, while the genitive noun
phrase is only optionally pronominalized.  This derivation shows that
the distinction izan$^\alpha$ and izan$^\beta$ is one merely of morphological convenience.

The sentences thus far derived contain what are traditionally
called *predicate nominatives*.  The attributive adjective construction is
derived from a relative construction that contains a predicate nominative in the relative clause.  This requires an application of R16 upon
the output of R18 with expanded constituents.

R18c(R16).  $^{np}$[$^{np}$[$^s$[N + Det. + PL + K - (N + Det. + PL + K') -
            Pred.Nom. + Det. + PL + K - izan + K + (K')]$^s$]$^{np}$
            $^{np}$[N + Det. + PL + X]$^{np}$]$^{np}$

This requires two readings:  one with the noun phrase marked with K'
and one without.

R18c(1). $\rightarrowtail$ $^{np}$[N$^1$ + Det. + PL + K - Pred.Nom. + Det. + PL + K -
            izan + K + Rel. - N$^1$ + Det. + PL + X]$^{np}$

R18c(2).  $^{np}$[N$^1$ + Det. + PL + K - N$^2$ + Det. + PL + K' -
            Pred.Nom. + Det. + PL + K - izan + K + K' + Rel. -
            N + Det. + PL + X]$^{np}$

In the first reading N$^1$ = N$^1$, while in the second the rightmost N must
be identical with the PP marked with K'.  This latter proviso is necessary to prevent the generation of the incoherent strings:

138a. *\*haren apheza den semea.*

138b. *\*aitak apheza duen semea.*

This rule does produce the following grammatical strings:

139. *ona den gizona.*

The man who is good.

140. *ontuak diren sagarrak.*

The apples that are ripe.

141. *serora den anderea.*

The lady who is a (religious) sister.

142. *zuhaitza den gizona.*

The man who is mean.

143. *semea apheza duen aita.*

The father whose son is a priest.

The attributive construction is derived by the following operation:

R18d. $^{np}$[Pred.Nom. + Det. + PL + K - izan + K + Rel. - Det. + PL + X] $\twoheadrightarrow$ $^{np}$[N + Pred.Nom. + Det. + PL + X]$^{np}$

By the application of this rule the following grammatical strings are generated:

144. *gizon ona*

The good man

145. *sagar ontuak*

The ripe apples

146. *andere serora*

Reverent sister

147. *gizon zuhaitza*

The mean man

Sentences 129, 130, 131 are derived by repeated applications of relativization and adjectivization transformations.

    3.005 The second major recursive device of this grammar is noun phrase complementation (2.032-2.035), where the complement is a sentence embedded in a structure of the form $^{np}$[$^{s}$[S]$^{s}$ + N + Det. + K]$^{np}$. Therefore, this construction is referred to as a noun phrase complementation or a completive. [S] is an expansion or modification of N + Det. In some sentences the complement sentence occupies the position of N + Det. For purposes of structural description we posit (PRO) for N + Det. In terms of strict case grammar, complement sentences are embedded directly under the O-node (Fillmore 1968:49). This we shall assume for the nuclear proposition (although Figure 42 superficially contradicts this assumption).   Characteristic of the noun phrase complement in Basque is that it is removed from the noun phrase and placed to the right of the nuclear proposition where it is affixed with a locative postposition.  In configurational terms, it is removed from the objective node and reassigned to a locative, i.e. lexical, node.

R19.   $^S[X - {}^{PP}[^S[S]^S - N + Det. + PL + K - Obj.]^{PP} - X]^S \twoheadrightarrow$

$^S[X^{PP}[N + Det. + PL + K - Obj.] - X - {}^{PP}[S - K - Loc.]^{PP}]^S$

In all cases the first realization of S - K - Loc. is *S-inessive* or, lexically, VC + *n*.  I make the strong claim that this termination, referred to as *conjunctive* in traditional grammars, is in the case of complementation the *-n* of the inessive case and that its phonetic identity with the -n of relativization and of the genitive is fortuitous. If the head of the noun phrase contains a feature [+ fact] another affix is attached to *(e)n*, *-la*.  By regular phonological development *-(e)n + la* becomes *(e)la*.  This implies that a string of this structural description without this feature on the head noun is marked [- fact].  Therefore, Rli will have two outputs:

R19a.  ... S-*(e)n*

R19b.  ... S-*(e)n* - *la*

These alternative readings account for the following sentences (2.034):

78.   *ez dut uste harena den.*

I do not believe it is his.

79.   *uste dut harena dela.*

I believe it is his.

Since Basque does not share negative raising with English, a factive sentence of the following form can be generated:

148.  *uste dut harena ez dela.*

I believe that it is not his.

In many cases of noun phrase complementation, such as those directly above, the head noun of the complementation is not present, and we must assume that the underlying N + Det. is vacuously filled with the

pronoun *hura*, for it is reflected in the finite verb form.   If the head
noun is present, i.e. in a truly completive construction, the complementation optionally takes on another form.   The input to this transformation is the output of R19b:

R19c.  $^S[X - ^{PP}[N + Det. + PL + K]^{PP} - X - S + ela]^S \twoheadrightarrow$

$^S[X - ^{PP}[S + ela + ko - N + Det. + PL + K]^{PP} - X]^S$

This will generate the grammatical sentence   (2.033):

69b.  *loterian irabazi dugulako berria duzu izan.*

You have had the news that we won in the lottery.

The third type of noun phrase complementation can be called shared-noun
noun phrase complementation (2.035).   In this case the embedded complement sentence shares one noun phrase with the matrix sentence and is of
a form that would be realized as, e.g.  [harek zu(re) ikusten zitu]
"He sees you."   It is embedded in a sentence, e.g. of the form  [ez dut
hura utzi] "I did not let him," where *hura = harek*.

R20.  $^S[(^{PP}[NP^2 - K]^{PP})\ ^{PP}[^S[^{PP}[NP^2 - K]^{PP}\ ^{PP}[NP^3 - K]^{PP}$

$^{vc}[Nom.Int. + inessive - finite verb]^{vc}]^S\ ^{PP}[NP^2 - K]^{np}$

$[VC]]^S \twoheadrightarrow {}^S[(^{PP}[NP^2 - K]^{PP})\ ^{PP}[NP^2 - K]\ ^{PP}[VC]\ ^{PP}[NP^3 +$

gen. - Nom.Int. + allative$]^{PP}]^S$

The application of this rule will produce the grammatical sentences
(2.035):

80.  *ez dut utzi zure ikistera.*

I did not let him see you.

81.  *entxeatu da jatera.*

He tried to eat.

The problem of whether the nominal complement (i.e. object) of the
nominal infinitive is marked neutral or genetive is a matter of dialect
detail (see Heath 1972).

3.006  Adnominal constructions are of two types, the possessive
or *en*-genitive and the locative or *ko*-genitive.   They are derived as
variations on the previously detailed embedding rules for relativization
and complementation.   Because the two adnominal constructions resemble
each other in their surface representations, they have both been dubbed

"genitives."  However, their derivational history is quite different.
They are both properly adnominal in that all propositional relationships have been removed from them, leaving them to be extrapolated from
context and from foreknowledge of the world.

The *en*-genitive is derived from various underlying structures.
One of these is the same structure that the relativizing transform
operates on in R.61.  However, the condition that generates a genitive
instead of a relative is the presence in the relativized embedded sentence of am empty verb (see Fillmore 1968:61-62).  The empty verb slot
is found in propositions that have in case grammar terms the structures
[NP + dat. - NP + neut. -____ ].  In Basque, the independently realized
sentence will be realized with the verb slot filled with transitive
*izan*$^{\beta}$ with the form [NP + erg. - NP + neut. - *izan*], e.g. *gizonak
muthikoa badut*.  Of course the common noun condition holds too.

R21(R16).  $^{PP}[^{PP}[^{S}[$NP + dat. - NP + neut. - $^{vc}[$ ____ $]^{vc}]^{s}]^{PP}$
$^{PP}[$N + Det. = X$]^{PP}]^{PP} \twoheadrightarrow {}^{PP}[$NP + Rel. - N + Det. - X$]^{PP}$

The relative -*en* replaces the case marked of the remaining NP.  Thus,
the exact relationship between the two noun phrases is obliterated.  The
possessive genitive termination is simply the relative -*en*.  The function of it is to show an undefined relationship between any two constituents.  As pointed out in 2.029, the exact relationship between the two
terms in *gizonaren muthikoa* remains undefined.

In the phrase *gizonaren semea* the underlying structure is different.  The first term is introduced not by embedding of a sentence, but
by a lexically determined specifying noun phrase.  That noun phrase
specifies the relationship of the head term to all members of its class,
in this case the natural system of kinship.  There are many such systems or natural classes, e.g. *gizonaren begia* "the man's eye," where the
part is related to the whole (of mammalian anatomy).  In the case of
part-to-whole relationships R21 is immensely simplified in that the
head noun extrudes its own specifier.

R21a.  $^{PP}[^{np}[$Specifier$]^{np}$ $^{PP}[$N + Det. + X$]^{PP} \twoheadrightarrow {}^{PP}[$Specifier +
Rel. - N + Det. + X$]^{PP}$

It is in this construction that the purely relational nature of *en* is
more apparent.

These genitives are generated also in other kinds of nominal
clauses (2.035, 2.032):

80.   *ez dut utzi zure ikustera.*

I did not let him see you.

66.   *Iaincoaren gureganaco charitatea.*

Charitas Dei in nobis.

The nominalized clauses in these sentences have the underlying form:

80a.  *harek zu ikhusi du.*

He has seen you.

66a.  *Iaincoak charitatea guregana badu.*

God has love for us.

In sentence 80 *zu*, as an independent neutral form of the pronoun is
demoted to a pure, i.e. empty relationship with the head of its construction *ikhusi* or, better, in terms of derivation, it was never assigned
the neutral case.  This is also true of *Iainco* in sentence 66.  With the
deletion of the noun shared by the constituent phrase and the matrix
phrase, the syntactic case-marker is realized by a relator, the *en*-
genitive.  In a number of nominalized clauses, nevertheless, uncertainty
prevails.

150.  *aita jiteaz kontent niz.*

150a. *aitaren jiteaz kontent niz.*

I am happy with father's coming.

(Speakers of English are equally uncertain about "with his coming" and
"with him coming.")

151.  *ura karreatzen ari du.*

151a. *uraren karreatzen ari da.*

He is (engaged in) carrying water.

Speakers are uncertain about just how the sentence is to be construed,
with or without embedding.  The situation in sentence 66 is much less
subject to a sort of equal probability interpretation.  In this case,
I shall use the complete quote with modernized orthography:

66b.  *Hunetan manifestatu izan da Jainkoaren gureganako karitatea,*
      *zeren bere Seme bakoitza igorri ukan baitu Jainkoak mundura*
      *hartzaz bizi garentzat.*

      In hoc apparuit caritas Dei in nobis, quoniam Filium suum
      unigenitum misit Deus in mundum, ut vivamus per eum.

Sentence 65 (2.032), given below also as a complete quote, shows that
*Jainkoaren gureganako karitatea* is a reduced relative clause.

65a.  *Eta guk ezagutu eta sinhetsi dugu Jainkoak guregana duen*
      *karitatea.*

      Et nos cognovimus et credidimus caritati, quam habet Deus
      in nobis.

The locative genetives mentioned above (2.030-31) display the same sort
of reduction:

58.   *ateko giltza*
      the door key

60.   *menditikako bidea*
      the road from the mountain

61.   *mendirako bidea*
      the road to the mountain.

These can be interpreted as reduced relative clauses, e.g.

58a.  *atetan dagon giltza*

The reduced relative is characterized by deletion of the verb complex
and by the indefiniteness of the noun and assignment to the locative.
Removal of the localizing constituents changes the form from individual
to generic.  In the New Testament quotes above, the translator makes a
neat distinction between God's general love for us and God's specific
acts of love.  (At least Leizarraga reads the text that way.)  Generic
reduction of relative constructions operates upon the output of R16
with an expansion of constituents and the feature indefinite upon the
shared noun in the constituent sentence.

        R22.  [(PRO) + X + nominal verb + finite verb + Rel. - N +
              Det. + Y] → [(PRO) + X + (nominal verb) + Ko + N +
              Det. + Y]

X can be filled with any noun phrase marked with a lexical case.  This
rule will produce such well-formed phrases as:

152.  *hik erosiko mandoa*

     the mule bought by you

This stands in contrast to a phrase such as:

153.  *hik erosi huen mandoa*

      the mule that you bought

The locative interpretation of the *ko*-genetive receives support from
parallel formations of the following type:

154.  *holako mandoa*

     that sort of mule

155.  *hemengo mandoa*

     the mule from here

The head noun of the construction is literally *located* in regard to all
other members of its class.  The locative genitive were better described
as the generic genitive in contrast to the specifying possessive genitive.  This is not derived from the meaning of *ko*, but from the structures that generate its occurrence.

    3.007  As I stressed very early in this essay, the purpose and
limits of this essay are closely confined to the categorial component
of Basque.  Consequently, little or no attention has been given to
important aspects of the grammar such as the lexicon (lexical cases,
the structure of the lexicon, morpheme structure rules, morphological
derivation), the verb complex (notably the modal particles *behar, ahal,
ari*), as well as negation and quantification.  It has been my aim to
arrive at significant generalizations that will contribute to the productive interpretation of those other parts of Basque grammar.  I
believe that I have demonstrated that the operative principle that
dominates the formation of all well-formed structures is the establishment of a modifying relationship between any two constituents on the
pattern of a modifier-modified (complement-head, specifier-specified).
It has been observed that most transformations, where two constituents
are turned into one, are repetitions of the same modifying operation

on structurally identical strings at varying levels, i.e. with progressive expansions of the constituents of a grammatical string, beginning
with the simplest proposition.  In impressionistic terms, the process
of sentence production proceeds not in a straight line, but in the
fashion of an arabesque by repetition of the same left-handed movement.
Even within my purposefully  narrow aims and restricted evidence, more
questions have been posed, adumbrated, and quietly ignored than have
been mentioned, examined, or tentatively answered.  Therefore, I entitled the essay *Prolegomena to a Grammar of Basque*.

# ENDNOTES

1. For an historical account of the Basque diaspora, see John Bilbao and William A. Douglass' *Amerikanuak: Basques in the New Yorld* (Reno: University of Nevada Press). Also see the section entitled "Basques in the New World" in Douglass 1977:7-70.

2. For a short account of the struggle for a unified literary language, see Luis Villasante, *Hacia la lengua literaria común* (serie "Luis de Elizalde" sobre unificación del euskera escrito). Basque aspirations to political independence have brought about a certain degree of unification at a very recent date.

3. See in particular N'Daiye 1970 and Gavel 1920.

4. Jonathan Seeley has given a concise history of the ergative problem in an article, "An ergative historiography," *Historiographia Linguistica* 4:191-206. In R. M. W. Dixon's admirable account of an ergative-type language of Australia, *The Dyirbal Language of North Queensland* (Cambridge: Cambridge University Press, 1972), there is a lucid discussion of the place of the ergative case in the framework of universal grammar. Another enlightening treatment of the ergative problem is to be found in Stephan Anderson's "On the notion of subject in ergative languages," in Li 1976:1-23. The whole question is treated in an arbitrary and doctrinaire manner by Eduard Keenan and Bernard Comris in "Noun phrase accessibility and universal grammar," *Linguistic Inquiry* 8 (1977):63-99. The treatment of the Basque materials is cavalier and shocking. In particular, the latter two studies try to set up as absolute metaphysical realities the traditional terms, subject and object, by means of a set of complex syntactic properties, tortuous to follow. Luckily, David E. Johnson published a brilliant refutation of this sort of argumentation, destroying it with impeccable logic, in "On Keenan's definition of 'subject-of'," *Linguistic Inquiry* 8 (1977):673-692.

5. The historical and morphological problems behind the fact that -*ak* is both ergative definite singular and neutral definite plural is discussed in great detail by William Jacobsen in "Ergative and nominative syncretism in Basque," *Anuario Urquijo*, pp. 67-109.

6.  See Wilbur 1975, 1978.

7.  The theory was first propounded by Stempf 1890.  It was further
    developed by Schuchardt 1893, 1923, and used systematically by
    Lafon 1943.  Although those grammarians seemed pleased with the
    theory, there was considerable resistance to it, particularly by
    native speakers, who found it counter-intuitive.  Lafitte rejects
    the theory (1962:342) with the words, "Cette théorie ingénieuse
    est une simple interprétation sans portée pratique, quoique très à
    la mode ches les bascologues."  The progress of the argument can
    be seen in Naert 1956, Martinet 1958, 1960, Lafon 1954, 1961.  I
    have for some time been at pains here and elsewhere to show that
    *les bascologues* were trying to shove the facts of Basque grammar
    into framework of an inadequate and inappropriate theory of grammar.
    See footnote 6, above.

8.  A particularly bad example of not understanding the passive voice
    is to be found in Bollenbacher's "The Basque passive," *Studies
    Bilbao*, pp. 181-192.  All of the sentences presented here as
    passive sentences are nothing but stative predicate adjective con-
    structions, which may seem to translate apparent passives in
    English.

9.  For these extensions of the theory, see Cook 1970, 1972.

10. R. P. G. de Rijk in "Partitive assignment in Basque," *Anuario
    Urquijo*, pp. 130-173, presents in lucid detail the conditions for
    the assignment of the partitive termination.  The most important
    accomplishment of this article is to separate *stative* from *parti-
    tive*.  They have always been hopelessly confounded in traditional
    Basque grammars.

11. Later developments in case grammar has posited additional roles,
    *goal, source, experiencer,* as well as *benefactive* and *deputive* to
    expand the possibilities that were originally subsumed under
    *dative*.  See Cook, footnote 9, above.  This extension of the origi-
    nal theory, if carried to its logical extreme, would find a differ-
    end role for every occurrence of every noun phrase with every verb
    that it might be construed with.

12. Since the appearance of Greenberg's original study of the uni-
    versals of word order in 1966, there have been various studies that
    have tested out the implications that Greenberg arrived at by
    empirical means.  R. P. G. de Rijk did this in 1969 with the facts
    of Basque word order.  Basque fits the SOV pattern rather well,
    complying dutifully to the implications with prenominal relative
    constructions, prenominal genitives, postpositions, and non-
    fronting of interrogatives.  Only the adjective does not fall into
    the otherwise fulfilled SOV pattern.  English likewise does not fit

the expected SVO adjective pattern.  My suspicion is that the
categorial role of the adjective has not been properly assessed.
Both in Basque and English the adjective-noun order reflects the
verb-object order, where object = noun, verb = adjective.  (This
turns traditional grammatical concepts upside down.)  In 1973
Vennemann refined and expanded Greenberg's hypotheses into a general
theory of language history on a cosmic scale.  My objection is that
S and O are taken as absolute entities with universal definitions.

13. The textual and contextual motivations for the rather free move-
    ment of the case-marked noun phrases within the Basque sentence
    cannot be defined within the narrow scope of a sentence grammar,
    which can tell us only what is well-formed and what is not.  Until
    an acceptable text theory is framed we shall have to be satisfied
    with the conveniently vague terms, *emphasis, focus, topic*.  Never-
    theless Donzead 1972 represents a nice step in the direction of a
    definition of the problem.

14. J. Anderson 1973 discusses in some detail the question of aspect in
    the inflection of the Basque verb.  These observations are of
    extreme importance for the final definition of a complete grammar
    of Basque.  Comrie 1976 shows us, however, that aspect is not so
    well understood as might be wished or so thoroughly as our own
    grammatical mythology would leads us to believe.  Until a compre-
    hensive and generally compelling theory of aspect is framed we
    shall have to be satisfied with such labels as *progressive, dura-
    tive, aorist, inchoative*, etc., hoping that everybody understands
    what we mean.

15. There. is no doubt that the theoretical position that permits us to
    set up this string would be better presented in the notation of
    categorial grammar, where grammatical strings are produced by
    repeated operations of the operator $\lambda$ upon diadyc strings of $\Sigma$ and
    $n$ .  Place-marking has in terms of such a grammar real rather than
    merely formal content in that the order of entrance of the consti-
    tuents into the derivation is dictated by the order of $\lambda$-binding.
    See Cresswell 1973, 1977.

# SELECT BIBLIOGRAPHY

Anderson, John. 1973. *An Essay Concerning Aspect*. (Janua Linguarum, series minor, 167.) The Hague: Mouton.

*Anuario del Seminario de Filología Vasca "Julio de Urquijo,"* Vol. VI, 1972. *Papers from the Basque Linguistics Seminar, University of Nevada, Summer 1972.* San Sebastián: Gráficas Colón.

Bilbao, Jon, and Douglass, William A. 1975. *Amerikanuak: Basques in the New Yorld*. Reno: University of Nevada Press.

Bollenbacher, John. 1977. "The Basque passive." Douglass 1977:181-192.

Chomsky, Noam. 1965. *Aspects of Syntax*. Cambridge, Mass.: MIT Press.

Cole, Peter, and Saddock, Jerrold, eds. 1977. *Syntax and Semantics*. Vol. 8. New York: Academic Press.

Comrie, Bernard. 1976. *Aspect*. Cambridge: Cambridge University Press.

Cook, Walter. 1970. "Case grammar: From roles to rules." *Languages and Linguistics Working Papers* 1:4-29.

_____. 1972. "A set of postulates for case grammar analysis." *Languages and Linguistics Working Papers* 4.

Cresswell, M. J. 1973. *Logic and Languages*. London: Methuen.

_____. 1977. *Categorial Languages*. Bloomington, Ind.: Indiana University Linguistics Club.

Dixon, R. M. W. 1972. *The Dyirbal Language of North Queensland*. Cambridge: Cambridge University Press.

Donzeau, Françoise. 1972. "The expression of focus in Basque." *Anuario Urquijo*, pp. 35-45.

Douglass, William, Etulain, Richard W., and Jacobsen, William H., eds. 1977. *Anglo-American Contributions to Basque Studies: Essays in Honor of John Bilbao*. Reno: University of Nevada Press.

Echaide, Ignacio. 1911. *Tratado de sufijación, prefijación y composición en el idioma euskaro*. San Sebastián: J. Baroja e Hijos.

_____. 1912. *Sintaxis del idioma euskaro*. San Sebastián: J. Baroja e Hijos.

Fillmore, Charles.  1968.  "The case for case."  In Emmon Bach and
     Robert T. Harms, eds.  *Universals in Linguistic Theory*.  New York:
     Holt, Rinehart & Winston.

_____.  1977.  "The case for case reopened."  Cole, pp. 59–87.

Finke, Peter.  1974.  *Theoretische Probleme der Kasusgrammatik*.  Kron-
     berg:  Scriptor Verlag.

Gavel, Henri.  1922.  *Eléments de phonétique basque*.  Paris:  Edouard
     Champion.  (Repr. as Vol. 12 of *Biblioteca de la Gran Enciclo-
     pedia Vasca*.)  Bilbao:  Editorial La Gran Enciclopedia Vasca.

Greenberg, Joseph H.  1966.  "Some universals of grammar with particu-
     lar reference to the order of meaningful elements."  In *Universals
     of Language*.  2nd ed.  Cambridge, Mass.:  MIT Press.

Holmer, Nils.  1964.  *El idioma vasco hablado.  Un estudio de dialecto-
     logía euskerica*.  San Sebastián:  Gráficas Izarra.

Jacobsen, William.  1972.  "Ergative and nominative syncretism in
     Basque."  *Anuario Urquijo*, pp. 67–109.

Johnson, David E.  1976.  *Toward a Theory of Relationally Based Grammar*.
     Bloomington, Ind.:  Indiana University Linguistics Club.

_____.  1977.  "On Keenan's definition of 'Subject of.'"  *Linguistic
     Inquiry* 8:673–692.

Keenan, Eduard, and Comrie, Bernard.  1977.  "Noun phrase accessibility
     and universal grammar."  *Linguistic Inquiry* 8:63–99.

Kimball, John P., ed.  1973.  *Syntax and Semantics*.  Vol. 2.  New York:
     Seminar Press.

Li, Charles N., ed.  1976.  *Subject and Topic*.  New York:  Academic
     Press.

Lafitte, Pierre.  1976.  *Grammaire basque (Navarro-Labourdin littéraire)*.
     Edition revue et corrigée.  Bayonne:  Editions des Amis du Musée
     Basque.

Lafon, René.  1943.  *Le système du verbe basque au XVI$^e$ siècle*.  2 vols.
     Bordeaux.

_____.  1947.  "Sur les suffixes *ti / tik*.  *Eusko-Jakintza* 1:141–150

_____.  1954.  "Comportement syntaxique, structure et diathèse du
     verbe basque."  *BSLP* 50:190–220.

_____.  1957.  "L'expression de la comparison en basque."  *BSLP*
     53:234–236.

_____.  1960.  "Sur les formes verbales basques qui contiennent un
     indice datif."  *BSLP* 55:139–162.

_____.  1961.  "L'expression de l'auteur de l'action en basque."
     *BSLP* 56:186–221.

Lakoff, George. 1970. *Irregularity in Syntax*. New York: Holt, Rinehart and Winston.

Lyons, John. 1968. *Introduction to Theoretical Linguistics*. Cambridge: Cambridge University Press.

_____. 1967. "A note on possessive, existential, and locative sentences." *Foundations of Language* 3:390-395.

Martin, William. 1972. *OWL* Automatic Programming Group, MIT. Cambridge, Mass.

Martinet, André. 1958. "La construction ergative et les structures élémentaires de l'énoncé." *Journal de Psychologie* 55:377-392.

_____. 1962. "Le sujet comme fonction linguistique et l'analyse syntaxique du basque." *BSLP* 57:73-102.

Michelena, Louis. 1961. *Fonética histórica vasca*. San Sebastián: Imprenta de la diputación de Guipúzcoa.

Naert, Pierre. 1956. "Le verbe basque, est-il passif?" *Studia Linguistica* 10:45-49.

N'Diaye, Geneviève. 1970. *Structure du dialecte basque de Maya*. (Janua Linguarum, series practice, 86.) The Hague: Mouton.

Ormaechea, Nicolás "Orixe", and Oyarzábal, Martín de. 1963. *El lenguaje vasco*. San Sebastián: Gráficas Izarra.

Rijk, R. P. G. de. 1969. "Is Basque an S.O.V. language? *Fontes Linguae Vasconum* 3:319-357.

_____. 1972. "Partitive assignment in Basque." *Anuario Urquijo*, pp. 130-173.

Robinson, Jane S. 1970. "Case, category, and configuration." *Journal of Linguistics* 6:57-80.

Schuchardt, Hugo Mario. 1893. *Baskische Studien I. Über die Entstehung der Bezugsformen des baskischen Zeitworts. Denkschriften der Akademie der Wissenschaften zu Wien* 42(no.3).

_____. 1923. *Primitiae linguae Vasconum*. Halle/Saale: Max Niemeyer.

Seeley, Jonathan. 1977. "An ergative historiography." *Historiographia Linguistica* 4:191-206.

Seuren, Pieter A. M. 1969. *Operators and Nucleus. A Contribution to the Theory of Grammar*. Cambridge: Cambridge University Press.

Stempf, Viktor. 1890. *Besitz die baskische Sprache ein transitives Zeitwort, oder nicht?* Bordeaux.

Tovar, Antonio. 1957. *The Basque Language*. Transl. by Herbert Pierrepont Houghton. Philadelphia: University of Pennsylvania Press.

Vennemann, Theo.  1975.  "Explanation in Syntax."  Kimball, pp. 1–50.

Villasante Cortabidarte, Luis, O.F.M.  1970.  *Hacia la lengua literaria commún*.  Serie "Luis de Elizalde" sobre unificatión del
euskera escrito.  Oñate (Guipúzcoa):  Editorial Franciscana
Aranzazu.

Wilbur, Terence H.  1970.  "Ergative and pseudo-ergative in Basque."
*Fontes Linguae Vasconum* 4:57–66.

_____.  1975.  "Transitive, intransitive, ergative:  A terminological
autopsy."  *Salzburger Beiträge zur Linguistik* 3:119–126. Tübingen.

_____.  1976.  "The causative construction in Basque."  *The Third
LACUS Forum 1976* 3:537–544.  Columbia, S.C.:  Hornbeam Press.

_____.  1977.  "The Basque proverb."  *The Fourth LACUS Forum 1977*
4:638–641.  Columbia, S.C.:  Hornbeam Press.

_____.  1977.  "The comparative construction in Basque."  Douglass
1977:177–180.

# APPENDIX I

## VOCABULARY

This appendix is intended to be a running checklist of lexical forms that occur in the text. After each item there is a categorial designation, e.g. V, N, ADJ, that will indicate the surface realizations in the text. As a matter of fact, it must be stressed that a Basque root belongs to no particular category aside from unique forms such as borrowings. Basque lexicographers will often gloss a root as "idea of...." This gloss will be followed by a very long entry that displays all the possible grammatical expansions and modifications of that root. See Lhande 1926 *passim*.

For every item labeled V, in the greater number of entries, two forms will be listed: the radical infinite and the perfect participle. In the case of idiosyncratic forms, e.g. *bizi*, only one form will be listed. Modal verbs or particles are listed in simple root form. All nouns are listed in the indefinite form.

*aberats* ADJ  rich

*abia, abiatu* V  to leave

*adi, aditu* V  to hear

*ahal* MOD V  to be able, can

*aho* N  mouth

*aintzin* N  front, previous time

*aise* ADV  easily, with ease

*aita* N  father

*akaba, akabatu* V  to end,
                    finish

*alde* N  side, beside

*aldiz* ADV  however, on the
             other hand

*alegrantze* N  happiness

*ama* N  mother

*anai* N  brother

*andere* N  woman, wife

*apez* N  priest

*apo* N  toad

*apur* N  scrap, small thing

*ardura* ADV  often

*argi* N  light

*argitu* V  to shine

*arizan* V  to mention

*arras, arrais* ADV  completely,
                     very
   *ez, ez arrais*  never

*arriba, arribatu* V  to arrive

*arropa* N  dress, clothing

*arte* PP  until, up to

*aski* ADJ, ADV  enough

*asma, asmatu* V  to guess, suppose

*atabal* N  drum

*ate* N  door, entrance

*atzeman, atxeman* V  to find,
                      catch

*azken* N, ADJ  last, end

*azpi* N  beneath, underside

*bainan* CONJ  but

*bake* N  peace

*bakotx, bakoitz* IND ADJ  each,
                           every

*bat* NUM  one

*batere* ADV  even

*batzu* ADJ  some

*begi* N  eye

*beha, behatu* V  to see, observe

*behar* MOD V  to have to, must

*behor(r)* N  mare

*bekatu* N  sin

*beldur(r)* N  fear

*beltz* ADJ  black

*benedika, benedikatu* V  to bless

*bere* PRO GEN 3d PERS REFL

*bere* ADJ the same

*berehala* ADV immediately

*berri* ADJ new

*berriz* ADV again

*bertze* ADJ other

*besti, bestitu* V to dress

*bezala* CONJ as, like

*bide* N toad, path

*bihi* N bit, single small thing

*borta* N door

*bota, botatu* V to throw

*botz* N voice

*buru* N head

*buruz* ADV ahead

*charitate.* N love, charity

*chuhur(r)* see *xuhur(r)*

*dantza* V N dance

*delibera* V to consider

*dembora* N time

*dio, diote* V see *jo, egin*

*diru* N money; see *sosa*

*duda* N doubt

*ebats, ebatsi* V to steal

*edan* V to drink

*eder(r)* ADJ beautiful

*eduki* V to keep, hold

*egin* V to make, to; auxiliary;
see *dio*, above.

*egoitza* N place to stay

*egon* V to remain

*ekhar(r), ekharri* V to carry,
transport

*eliza* N church

*eman* V to give

*ene* PRO GEN my

*entseatu, entxeatu* V to try,
attempt

*erabil, erabili* V to push, cause
to walk; see
*ibili*.

*erdi* N, ADJ half

*eri* ADJ ill, sick

*eritasun* N illness

*eros, erosi* V to buy

*erran* V to say

*eskuta, eskutatu* V to listen, hear

*espantu* ADJ proud, bragging

*espartin* N sandal

*eta* CONJ and

*etor(r), etorri* V to come

*etsamina, etsaminatu* V to examine

*etze* N house, home

*ez* ADV not, no

*ezagu, ezagutu* V to be acquainted with, know

*ezagutze* N acquaintance

*ezarri* V to don, dress, put on

*ezin* MOD PART not able

*fama* N rumor

*familia* N family

*fusta* N onomatopoetic word "whoosh"

*gabe* PP without

*gain* N top

*gaindi* PP by way of

*gal, galdu* V to lose

*galdegin* V to ask

*galtzagorri* N devil

*gana* PP toward

*garbi* ADJ clean

*garbi, garbitu* V to clean

*gauerdi* N midnight

*gaur* N, ADV night, tonight

*gero* ADV then

*gerta, gertatu* V to happen

*gertakaria* N silly happening

*giltz* N key

*gizon* N man

*gorde* V to hide

*gosa, gosatu* V to enjoy

*gure* PRO GEN our

*guti* N small amount

*gutiago* ADV, ADJ less

*guzi* ADK all, every

*hainbertze* ADV so much

*halere* ADV nevertheless

*hamalau* NUM fourteen

*han* ADV there

*handi, haundi* ADJ big

*har, hartu* V to take

*harrama* N noise

*harri* N stone

*has, hasi* V to begin

*hatzeman* V to find, catch; see *atzeman*

*haur(r)* N child

*heben* ADV see *hemen*

*hel, heldu* V to come

*hemen, heben* ADV here

*higuin* V to dislike, be disgusted by

*hire* PRO your 2d sg fam.

*hiri* N town, village

*hitzeman* V to promise

*hobeago* ADJ, ADV better; see
   *on, un, huna*

*hola* ADV in this manner

*holako* ADJ of such a nature,
   such and such

*hun* DEM 3rd PERS

*huna* V *voilà*

*hur* N water; also *ur*

*hurus* ADJ happy

*husta* N onomatopoetic word
   "shoosh"

*igor(r), igorri* V to send

*iguzki* N sun

*ihardets, ihardesti* V to
   answer

*ikus, ikusi* V to see

*irabazi* V to win

*izan* V to have, to be; general
   auxiliary

*jainko* N God; see *jinko,
   jaingoikoa*

*jakin* V to know

*jan* V to eat

*janarazi* V to cause to eat,
   feed

*jauts (jaits), jautsi* V to
   descent, go down,
   come down

*jin* V to come

*jinko* N God

*jo* V to hit, strike, say

*joan* V to go

*karga, kargatu* V to load, charge,
   be pregnant

*komertzari* N business

*kontent* ADJ content

*kurri, kurritu* V to run about,
   circulate

*laket* V to please

*laster(r)* ADJ, ADV quick, fast

*leinu* N descendant

*leku* N place, location

*liboru* N book

*lo* V to sleep

*loteri* N lottery

*lotu* V to attack, befall

*maite* ADJ dear

*mana, manatu* V to order

*manamendu* N order

*mando* N mule

*mandozain* N mule-driver

*mendi* N mountain

*merkatu* N market

*mespresio* N disdain, hatred

*mia, miatu* V to see, look observe

*mintzo, mintzatu* V to speak

*mutiko* N boy

*nagusi* N boss, owner; pl. *Herr-schaften*

*nahi* MOD V to want, wish

*nahi* N desire

*nola* INT how

*non* INT where

*norbait* IND PRO someone

*ogi* N bread, wheat

*ohoin* N thief

*oihan* N forest

*on* ADJ good; also *un, hun*

*ontsa* ADV well

*orai* ADV now

*oraino* ADV again, still

*orduko* ADV again, still

*oro* ADV all, totally

*otoi* N prayer, "please"

*otoiz, otoizt* V to ask, pray

*paga, pagatu* V to pay

*pario* N bet, wager

*parti, partitu* V to depart

*pasa, pasatu* V to pass, pass through

*pekatu* N sin; see *bekatu*

*pena* N pain, moral pain

*pentsa, pentsatu* V to think

*piajant* N pilgrim

*plazer* V, N to be pleased with; pleasure

*puxka* N piece, small portion

*sarrarazi* V to cause to enter

*seme* N son

*senda, sendatu* V to heal, become well

*sendarazi* V to heal, cause to become well

*senar(r)* N husband

*sorgin* N witch

*soinu* N music

*tamburina* N tambourine

*trebesa, trebesatu* V to cross over

*trompa, trompatu* V to dupe, fool

*ttiki* ADJ small, little

*ur, hur* N water

*urde* N pig

*urte* N year

*urdina* ADJ blue

*uts, uste* V to believe

*utz, uztu* V to let, permit

*utzi*

*uxa, uxatu* V to push

*xuhuers* N scarce, parsimo-
nious, frugal;
cf. *zuhurer*

*xuxen*        see *zuzen*

*zabal* N, ADJ broad, wide

*zagar(r)* N apple

*zahar(r)* ADJ old

*zakur(r)* N dog; also *xakur(r)*

*zazpi* NUM seven

*zer* INT what

*zeren ... bait* CONJ because; see
also *-kotz*

*zeru* N heaven, sky

*zombait* IND some, few

*zubi* N bridge

*zuhur(r)* ADJ wise, prudent

*zure* PRO GEN your; 2d sg form

*zuren* PRO GEN your; 2nd pl form

*zuzen* ADJ straight, honest

# APPENDIX II

## Inflected Verb Forms

For the convenience of the reader, I have listed in alphabetical order all of the inflected verb forms that occur in the text. Each form is provided with an analysis of its morphemic content, i.e. connectives, pronominal reflexes, tense indicators, root. This is followed by a designation of tense and mood of the verbal form. Since the greater number of these forms will be inflected forms of the general verbal auxiliary, *izan*, transitive and intransitive, there will be no indication of the source verb. In the cases of other auxiliaries and the root-inflecting verbs, the source verb will be indicated in parentheses directly after the inflected form. Participial forms of the compound verbs will be listed after the entry that analyzes its auxiliary. e.g. *baitzuen:* CONN-3E-3N-R/ PAST-IND; *trompatu:* PERF-PART/ PAST IND. This is to be read: "connective-third singular ergative-third singular neutral-root/ past indicative; *trompatu:* perfect participle/ past indicative." The participial forms will be defined in the glossary, Appendix I. This list of forms is by no means intended to be an explanation of the complex and often capricious Basque verb.

The abbreviations used in the instant analyses of the verbal forms are as follows:

    1 = first person singular
    1P = first person plural
    2 = second person singular
    2M = second person singular masculine

```
2F  = second person singular feminine
2P  = second person singular formal
2PP = second person plural formal
3   = third person singular
```
It must be noted that indications of plurality are sometimes ambiguous and sometimes redundant.  Entries will at times read "3N ... 3NP" or "3E ... P" or "2P ... P."  This latter possibility leads to the creation of ambiguous forms such as *diote* "They have it for him" or "He has it for them," where the plural indicator, *te*, can be construed with 3D or 3E.

```
AL   = allocutive.  ALM = allocutive second singular masculine.
       ALF = allocutive second singular feminine.  ALFORM =
       allocutive second singular formal.  ALFORMP = allocutive
       second person plural formal
COMP = complementizer
COND = conditional
CONN = connective
D    = dative
DET  = determinative
EL   = elative postposition
E    = ergative
FUT  = future suffix
IMP  = imperative
IN   = inessive postposition
IND  = indicative
INST = instrumental postposition
INT  = interrogative suffix
MOD  = modal verb
NEG  = negative prefix
N    = neutral
PAST = past tense
```

```
POS  = positive prefix
POT  = potential mood
PRES = present tense
R    = root
RAD  = radical infinitive
REL  = relativizer
SUBJ = subjunctive
SUP  = suppositive
```

| | |
|---|---|
| *badea* | POS-3N-R-INT/ PRES-IND-INT |
| *baditu* | POS-3N-3NP-R-3E/ PRES-IND |
| *badoha (joan)* | POS-3N-4/ PRES-IND |
| *badohazi (joan)* | POS-3N-R-3NP/ PRES-IND |
| *badut* | POS-3N-R-1E/ PRES-IND |
| *baduzu* | COND-3N-R-2PE/ PRES-IND |
| *baitziren* | CAUS-3N-R/ PAST-IND |
| *baitzuen* | CAUS-3E-3N-R/ PAST-IND |
|    *trompatu* | PART-PERF/ PAST-IND |
| *balitu* | COND-3E-3N-3NP-R/ SUP |
| *baziren* | POS-3N-3NP-3-PAST/ PAST-IND |
| *bazituztela* | POS-3E-3N-3NP-R-3NP-3EP-PAST-COMP/ PAST-IND |
| *bazituzten* | POS-3E-3N-3NP-4-3NP-3EP-PAST/ PAST-IND |
| *beha (behatu)* | R/ IMP |
| *da* | 3N-R/ PRES-IND |
|    *argitzen* | PRES-PART-IN/ PRES-PROG-IND |
|    *entxeatu* | PERF-PART/ PRES-PERF-IND |
|    *etorri* | PERF-PART/ PRES-PERF-IND |
|    *galdu* | PRES-PART/ PRES-PERF-IND |
|    *heltzen* | PERF-PART-IN/ PRES-PROG-IND |
|    *joan* | PERF-PART/ PRES-PERF-IND |
| *dago (egon)* | 3N-R/ PRES-IND |
| *dagoka (eduki)* | 3N-R-3E/ PRES-IND |
| *dagokan (eduki)* | 3N-R-3E-REL/ PRES-IND |
| *dakit (jakin)* | 3N-R-1E/ PRES-IND |

| | | |
|---|---|---|
| *daut* | 3N-R-1D-3E/ PRES-IND | |
| *erran* | PERF-PART/ PRES-PERF-IND | |
| *heltzen* | PRES-PART-IN/ PRES-PROG-IND | |
| *dela* | 3N-R-REL-COMP/ PRES-IND | |
| *den* | 3N-R-REL/ PRES-IND | |
| *chuhurtuko* | PERF-PART-FUT/ FUT-IND | |
| *etorriko* | PERF-PART-FUT/ FUT-IND | |
| *gertatzen* | PRES-PART-IN/ PRES-PROG-IND | |
| *denik* | 3N-R-REL-EL/ PRES-IND | |
| *heldu* | PERF-PART/ PRES-PERF-IND | |
| *dezadan* | 3N-4-1E-REL/ PRES-SUBJ | |
| *dezakete* | 3N-R-POT-3E-3EP/ PRES-POT-SUBJ | |
| *diat* | 3N-R-ALM-2E/ PRES-IND | |
| *jakin* | PERF-PART/ PRES-PERF-IND | |
| *dio (egin)* | 3N-R-3E-3E/ PRES-IND | |
| *erraiten* | PRES-PART-IN/ PRES-PROG-IND | |
| *dio (jo)* | 3N-R-3E/ PRES-IND | |
| *diote (egin)* | 3N-R-3D-3PE/ PRES-IND | |
| *erraiten diote* | PRES-PART-IN/ PRES-PROG-IND | |
| *diote (jo)* | 3N-R-3E-3EP/ PRES-IND | |
| *dira, dire* | 3N-R-3NP/ PRES-IND | |
| *etortzen* | PRES-PART-IN/ PRES-PROG-IND | |
| *jin* | PERF-PART/ PRES-PERF-IND | |
| *diren* | 3N-R-3NP-REL/ PRES-IND | |
| *dituen* | 3N-3NP-R-3E-REL/ PRES-IND | |

*ditut*                   3N-3NP-R-1E/ PRES-IND

   *higuintzen*              PRES-PART-IN/ PRES-PROG-IND

*dituzte*                 3N-3NP-R-3NP-3E-3EP/ PRES-IND

   *ezarten*                 PRES-PART-IN/ PRES-PROG-IND

*du*                      3N-R-3E/ PRES-IND

   *argitzen*                PRES-PART-IN/ PRES-PROG-IND

   *galdu*                   PERF-PART/ PRES-PERF-IND

   *ikusi*                   PERF-PART/ PRES-PERF-IND

   *jan*                     PERF-PART/ PRES-PERF-IND

   *joan*                    PERF-PART/ PRES-PERF-IND

   *kurritzen*               PRES-PART-IN/ PRES-PROG-IND

   *manatu*                  PERF-PART/ PRES-PERF-IND

*duela*                   3N-R-3E-REL-COMP/ PRES-IND

*duen*                    3N-R-3E-REL/ PRES-IND

   *ikusi*                   PERF-PART/ PRES-PERF

*dugu*                    3N-R-2EP/ PRES-IND

   *miatu behar*             PERF-PART-MOD/ PRES-MOD-IND

*dugula, dugulako*        3N-R-1EP-COMP-(COMP)

   *irabazi*                 PERF-PART/ PRES-PERF-IND

*dugun*                   3N-R--EP-REL/ PRES-IND

   *erraiten*                PRES-PART-IN/ PRES-PROG-IND

*duk*                     3N-R-2EM/ PRES-IND

   *jakinen*                 PERF-PART-GEN/ FUT-IND

*dut*                     3N-R-2E/ PRES-IND

   *ikusi*                   PERF-PART/ PRES-PERF-IND

| | |
|---|---|
| *kurritu* | PER-PART/ PRES-PERF-IND |
| *laket* | PERF-PART/ PRES-PERF-IND |
| *uste* | PERF-PART/ PRES-PERF-IND |
| *utzi* | PERF-PART/ PRES-PERF-IND |
| *dute* | 3N-R-3EP/ PRES-IND |
| *hatzeman* | PERF-PART/ PRES-PERF-IND |
| *nahi* | MOD/ PRES-IND |
| *sendaraziko* | PERF-PART-FUT/ FUT-IND |
| *duzu* | 3N-R-2PE/ PRES-IND |
| *izan* | PERF-PART/ PRES-PERF-IND |
| *duzuea* | 3N-R-2EP-P-INT/ PRES-IND |
| *nahi* | MOD/ PRES-IND |
| *etzaion* | NEG-3N-R-3D-PAST/ PAST-IND |
| *etzakien* | NEG-3E-3N-R-PAST/ PAST-IND |
| *etzare, etzire* | NEG-3N-R-3NP/ PRES-IND |
| *sendatuko* | PERF-PART-FUT/ FUT-IND |
| *etzen* | NEG-*zen*; see below |
| *etzuen* | NEG-*zuen*; see below |
| *ezbaitzen* | NEG-CONN-3N-R-PAST/ PAST-IND |
| *ezdakiena (jakin)* | NEG-3N-R-REL-DET/ PRES-IND |
| *ezdakit (jakin)* | NEG-*dakit*; see above |
| *ezdut* | NEG-*dut uste*; see above |
| *gaiten* | 2PN-R-O-REL/ PRES-SUBJ |
| *jaits (jauts)* | RAD/ PRES-SUBJ |

*nezake*              1E-3N-R-POT/

  *egin*                  RAD/ PRES-POT-SUBJ

*nintzen*             2N-R-PAST/ PAST-IND

  *bizi*                 PRES-PART/ PAST-PROG-IND

*nituen*              1E-3N-3NP-R-PAST/ PAST-IND

*nituen*              2E-3N-3NP-R-PAST-REL/ PAST-IND

  *hatxemanen*             PERF-PART-FUT/ FUT-IND

*nu*                  2N-R-3E/ PRES-IND

  *ikusi*               PERF-PART/ PRES-PERF-IND

*zaio*                3N-R-3D/ PRES-IND

  *laketzen*            PRES-PART-IN/ PRES-PROG-IND

*zaitugu*             2NP-2NP-R-PE/ PRES-IND

*zaizkit*             3N-R-3NP-2D/ PRES-IND

  *higuintzen*             PRES-PART-IN/ PRES-PROG-IND

*zaizkon*             3N-R-3NP-3D-3E-PAST/ PAST-IND

  *eman*                 PERF-PART/ PAST-IND

  *hitzeman*             PERF-PART/ PAST-IND

*zaizkona*            3N-R-3NP-3D-3E-PAST-REL-DEM

  *ebatzi*               PERF-PART/ PAST-IND

*zaiztan*             3N-R-3NP-2D-PAST/ PAST-IND

*zazaten*             3E-3N-R-3EP-PAST-REL/ PAST-SUBJ

  *jo*                  RAD/ PAST-SUBJ

*zazue*               3N-R-2PE-P/ IMP

  *pentsa*               RAD/ IMP

| | |
|---|---|
| *zela* | 3N-R-PAST-REL-COMP/ PAST-IND |
| *jin* | PERF-PART/ PAST-IND |
| *zelako* | 3N-R-PAST-REL-COMP-(COMP) |
| *jin* | see above |
| *zen* | 3N-R-PAST/ PAST-IND |
| *akabatu* | PERF-PART/ PAST-IND |
| *arribatu* | PERF-PART/ PAST-IND |
| *bestitu* | PERF-PART/ PAST-IND |
| *bizi* | PRES-PART/ PAST-PROG-IND |
| *etorri* | PERF-PART/ PAST-IND |
| *hasi* | PERF-PART/ PAST-IND |
| *joan* | PERF-PART/ PAST-IND |
| *partitu* | PERF-PART/ PAST-IND |
| *zezok* | 3N-R-3D-2EM/ IMP |
| *galda* | RAD/ IMP |
| *zinuela* | PE-R-PAST-REL-COMP/ PAST-IND |
| *botatu* | PERF-PART/ PAST-IND |
| *zioen* | 3E-3N-R-3D-PAST-REL/ PAST-IND |
| *erran* | PERF-PART/ PAST-IND |
| *zion* | 3E-3N-R-3D-PAST/ PAST-IND |
| *erran* | PERF-PART/ PAST-IND |
| *ihardetsi* | PERF-PART/ PAST-IND |
| *zioten* | 3E-3N-R-3D-3EP-PAST or<br>3E-3N-R-3D-3DP-PAST/PAST-IND |
| *erran* | PERF-PART/ PAST-IND |

| | |
|---|---|
| *ziotenez* | 3E-3N-R-3D-3EP-PAST-REL-INST/ PAST-IND |
| *eman nahi* | PERF-PART-MOD/ PAST-MOD-IND |
| *zira* | 2NP-R/ PRES-IND |
| *zirea* | 2NP-R-INT/ PRES-IND |
| *orhoitzen* | PRES-PART/ PRES-PROG-IND-INT |
| *zirela* | 2NP-R-PAST-REL-COMP/ PAST-IND |
| *ziren* | 2NP-R-PAST/ PAST-IND |
| *(dantzan) eman* | PERF-PART/ PAST-IND |
| *(egiten) eman* | see above |
| *galdu* | PERF-PART/ PAST-IND |
| *heltzen* | PRES-PART-IN/ PAST-PROG-IND |
| *jautsi jautsiak* | PERF-PART-PERF-PART-DEM-PL/ PAST-IND |
| *joaiten* | PRES-PART-IN/ PAST-PROG-IND |
| *zirenean* | 2NP-R-PAST-REL-DEM-IN/ PAST-IND |
| *gosatu* | PERF-PART/ PAST-IND |
| *zitakela* | 3NP-R-POT-PAST-REL-COMP/ PAST-POT-IND |
| *zitu, zaitu* | 2NP-2NP-R-3E/ PRES-IND |
| *ikusten* | PRES-PART-IN/ PRES-PROG-IND |
| *zituela* | 3E-3N-3NP-R-PAST-REL-COMP/ PAST-IND |
| *galdu* | PERF-PART/ PAST-IND |
| *izanen* | PERF-PART-FUT/ PAST-PROG-IND |
| *zituen* | 3E-3N-3NP-R-PAST/ PAST-IND |
| *aditu* | PERF-PART/ PAST-IND |
| *lotu* | PERF-PART/ PAST-IND |

| | |
|---|---|
| *zituen* | 3E-3N-3NP-R-PAST-REL/ PAST-IND |
| *nahi* | MOD/ PAST-MOD-IND |
| *zituztela* | 3E-3N-3NP-R-3NP-3EP-PAST-REL-COMP/ PAST-IND |
| *egin* | PERF-PART/ PAST-IND |
| *zuen* | 3E-3N-R-PAST/ PAST-IND |
| *deliberatu* | PERF-PART/ PAST-IND |
| *egiten* | PRES-PART-IN/ PAST-PROG-IND |
| *erraiten* | PRES-PART-IN/ PAST-PROG-IND |
| *eskutatu* | PERF-PART/ PAST-IND |
| *etsaminatu* | PERF-PART/ PAST-IND |
| *ikusten* | PRES-PART-IN/ PAST-PROG-IND |
| *irabazi* | PERF-PART/ PAST-IND |
| *jakin* | PERF-PART/ PAST-IND |
| *jo* | PERF-PART/ PAST-IND |
| *kurritu* | PERF-PART/ PAST-IND |
| *trebesatu behar* | PERF-PART-MOD/ PAST-MOD-IND |
| *zuena* | 3E-3N-R-PAST-REL-DET/ PAST-IND |
| *galdu* | PERF-PART/ PAST-IND |
| *zuenak* | 3E-3N-R-PAST-REL-DEM-PL/ PAST-IND |
| *galtzen* | PRES-PART-IN/ PAST-PROG-IND |
| *zutela* | 3E-3N-R-3EP-PAST-REL-COMP/ PAST-IND |
| *iardets ezin* | PERF-PART-MOD/ PAST-MOD-IND |
| *galdu* | PERF-PART/ PAST-IND |

| *zuten* | 3E-3N-R-3EP-PAST/ PAST-IND |
| *botatu* | PERF-PART/ PAST-IND |
| *egin* | PERF-PART/ PAST-IND |
| *garbitu* | PERF-PART/ PAST-IND |
| *hatxeman* | PERF-PART/ PAST-IND |
| *sarrarazi* | PERF-PART/ PAST-IND |
| *zuten* | 3E-3N-R-3EP-PAST-REL/ PAST-IND |
| *erran* | PERF-PART/ PAST-IND |
| *igorri* | PERF-PART/ PAST-IND |